ESSENTIAL ENGLISH SERIES

English Commercial Practice and Correspondence

Other books by
C. E. ECKERSLEY AND W. KAUFMANN

English and American Business Letters
A Commercial Course for Foreign Students   Volume 1
A Commercial Course for Foreign Students   Volume 2
with A. H. Elliott

ESSENTIAL ENGLISH SERIES

English Commercial Practice and Correspondence

A First Course for Foreign Students

C. E. ECKERSLEY and
W. KAUFMANN
Illustrations by Graham

Longman

LONGMAN GROUP LIMITED
London

*Associated companies, branches and representatives
throughout the world*

© Longman Group Ltd 1963, 1973

All rights reserved. No part of this publication may be
reproduced, stored in a retrieval system, or transmitted
in any form or by any means—electronic, mechanical,
photocopying, recording, or otherwise—without the
prior permission of the Copyright owner.

First published 1952
New edition 1963
New impressions *1965 (twice); *1967;
*1969 (twice); *1970 (twice):
New edition 1973
Second impression 1974
New impression *1975

ISBN 0 582 55230 3

Printed in Hong Kong by
The Continental Printing Co Ltd

Preface

There is, we believe, a real need for a book to give the *foreign* student, simply and clearly, the outlines of English commercial practice and guidance on the writing of business letters. There are numerous admirable books for this purpose for the *English* student, but his problems and difficulties are not generally those of the foreign student. It is to meet the particular needs of the non-English student that the present book has been written.

A glance at the Contents list will show that the main branches of English commercial practice are dealt with, and, after an account of the work of each department, specimens of correspondence relevant to its activities are given. In this connection readers should note a special feature (not, so far as we know, to be found in any other book of this kind), the Appendix of Standard Phrases for Correspondence (pages 232-46). So often the student, confronted with the problem of writing business letters, is at a loss to know what is the appropriate expression for his particular type of letter. He will, it is true, have met all these expressions as he has worked through the book, but until he has had considerable experience in the writing of letters, the right phrase may not necessarily rise to his call when he wants it. In the Appendix he will find the various alternatives all ready classified to help him out of this difficulty.

Our aim, however, has been not only to teach him English commercial practice, but also to teach him *English*, to enlarge his general vocabulary, to exercise him in grammatical construction and to increase his powers of expressing himself in English with ease and clearness. So, each chapter is followed by two types of exercises, the first to develop his command of the language, the second to consolidate the technical material he has just studied and to drill him in the practical matters of business life. In these exercises the phonetic transcription is given of certain words whose pronunciation might cause the student some difficulty. A brief guide to the phonetic symbols is given in Appendix II, p. 247.

Every attempt has been made to ensure that the book is an accurate picture of English business life today. But we have tried, too, to make the book pleasant and lively as well as useful, and, in following the progress of our friend Olaf (well-known to readers of *Essential English*[1]) through the various departments of a business firm,[2] to give a touch of human interest and reality to a subject that, in so many textbooks, tends to become dull and unreal. In this attempt at a "Brighter Commercial Course" we have had invaluable support from our artist, "Graham", one of the best known cartoonists of the day, who has given his witty interpretation (or misinterpretation!) of various expressions that he met in these pages. In doing so he has reminded us, and may help our readers to learn (with a smile, we hope,) that English words and phrases are not always limited to just one meaning.

The vocabulary of this book, apart from technical terms, is based on the 2,000 words of *Essential English*. These technical terms are given at the head of each chapter and their meaning and use are made clear in the text.

Students who have mastered this present book will find they are now able to study the subject in more detail and at a more advanced level in *A Commercial Course for Foreign Students*, Vols. 1 and 2.

C. E. E.
W. K.

[1] *Essential English for Foreign Students*, Books I-IV, by C. E. Eckersley (Longman).
[2] Some readers may feel that, as the organisation of only one type of firm (Weavewell Woollen Co.) is studied in this book, their particular requirements are not dealt with. But the organisation of all business firms, no matter what commodity they deal in, is fundamentally the same. It is only the technical vocabulary, peculiar to each trade, that will be different. The reader will, perhaps, notice that in the exercises an attempt has been made to bring in the vocabulary of a variety of trades.

Contents

		page
1.	OLAF BEGINS WORK	1
2.	TRAVELLING TO THE CITY	4
3.	HOW OLAF GOT HIS JOB	7
4.	OLAF WRITES TO HIS FATHER	14
5.	CONFIRMING AN APPOINTMENT	16
6.	THE MANAGER'S ROOM	18
7.	THE GENERAL OFFICE	20
8.	FILING	24
9.	THE OFFICE EQUIPMENT	30
10.	THE TELEPHONE SWITCHBOARD	35
11.	THE WORK OF THE GENERAL OFFICE	40
12.	COMMERCIAL CORRESPONDENCE	45
13.	APPLICATIONS FOR A JOB	53
14.	THE SALES DEPARTMENT	60
15.	CORRESPONDENCE OF THE SALES DEPARTMENT (1)	64
16.	CORRESPONDENCE OF THE SALES DEPARTMENT (2)	72
17.	SOME EXPLANATIONS. SALES PROMOTION	84
18.	A CIRCULAR AND THE INQUIRIES FROM IT	90
19.	ORDERS AND THEIR EXECUTION	97
	Correspondence	97
20.	COMPLAINTS, APOLOGIES AND ADJUSTMENTS	118
	Correspondence	119
21.	THE WAREHOUSE AND THE BUYER	135
	Correspondence	141
22.	INVOICES	146

	page
23. DEBIT AND CREDIT NOTES, DELIVERY ORDERS AND ADVICE NOTES	154
24. ACCOUNTS (1)	162
25. ACCOUNTS (2)	170
Correspondence	172
26. STATISTICS	188
27. THE EXPORT DEPARTMENT	193
Correspondence	197
28. THE BILL OF LADING (B/L)	202
Correspondence	204
29. THE BILL OF EXCHANGE (B/E)	208
Correspondence	214
30. THE LETTER OF CREDIT (L/C)	222
Correspondence	226
CONCLUSION	230
APPENDIX I	232
Standard Phrases for Correspondence	
APPENDIX II	247
Guide to Phonetic Transcription	
INDEX	248

1
Olaf Begins Work

**calendar   employment   company   clerk   office
business   manager**

As Olaf opened his eyes about seven o'clock in the morning, he looked at the calendar by his bedside. OCTOBER it said. And round today's date 'Monday, 19' was a red ring. It was an important date in his life. Today he was starting work. For two years he had been a student with Mr. Priestley[1] learning English, but all that was over now. Today he was going to begin to earn his own living. Today he was to begin his employment in the office of the Weavewell Woollen Co. Ltd. as a junior clerk. He knew very little about office work—hardly anything at all—but he had quite a good knowledge of English now, he was intelligent, he meant to work hard and to learn all he could.

He jumped out of bed, shaved and bathed quickly and came back to his bedroom to dress. 'No,' he thought, 'I can't wear the sports jacket and flannel trousers that I wore at Mr. Priestley's. I am a business man now; I'm "something in the City".[2] I know business men of today don't all wear the bowler hats, black coats and striped trousers that they once wore, but I don't think the Manager of Weavewell's office would like me to come in a sports jacket.' So he put on a dark grey suit with a white shirt and collar, a quiet silk tie of red and grey, black socks and shoes. The day was rather cold so, as soon as he had

---

[1] See *Essential English*, Books I-IV.

[2] 'The City' is the square mile between the Thames in the South and London Wall in the North, between the Strand in the West and Tower Hill in the East. This is the commercial and financial heart of London and of England.

finished his breakfast, he put on his dark blue overcoat, his hat and gloves, and with his morning paper (*The Times*) under his arm he set off for the station.

Exercises

I WORD STUDY. *Use each of the following words, taken from Chapter I, in sentences of your own:*

calendar, earn, employment (use also *employ, employer, employee, unemployment, the unemployed*), junior (what is the opposite?), clerk (note the pronunciation. In England it is generally [klɑːk], in U.S.A. it is [kləːrk]), hardly (what is the difference between 'he works hard' and 'he hardly works'?), intelligent (use also *unintelligent*, and *intelligence*), bath (noun and verb. Use also *bathe* pronunciation [beið]), flannel (mention three other materials from which clothes are made), striped (be careful with the pronunciation [straipt]), business (note the pronunciation ['biznis]), manager (use also *management*), grey (mention eight other colours), socks (what is the difference between *socks* and *stockings*? Name six articles of men's clothing and six of women's), breakfast (mention the other meals).

II IDIOMS. *Explain:*

1. all that *was over* now; 2. he *meant to* work hard; 3. a *quiet* silk tie (note the pronunciation of *quite* [kwait] and *quiet* ['kwaiət]); 4. he *set off for* the station; 5. he was *going to* begin to earn his living; 6. he *was to begin* his employment.

III *Make the following sentences negative:*

1. Olaf opened his eyes. 2. He looked at the calendar. 3. It was an important date. 4. He had been a student for two years. 5. He knew a great deal about office work. (Use *much* for *a great deal* in the negative.) 6. He meant to work hard. 7. He can wear a sports jacket at the office. 8. He could wear flannel trousers in the City. 9. He wore a sports jacket at Mr. Priestley's. 10. Olaf knows some business men. (*Some* will be *any* in the negative.) 11. Olaf put on a dark suit. 12. Olaf puts on his overcoat. 13. The manager would like to see me come in a sports jacket.

IV *Answer the following:*

1. What is a calendar? 2. Give, in English, the names of (a) the months of the year, (b) the days of the week. 3. What is a junior clerk? 4. What work do you think a junior clerk will do? 5. How is Olaf going to earn his living? 6. How do you earn your living?

2
Travelling to the City

typist   secretary   bank

Though a great many people in London work in the City, very few people live in it. They live in the 'suburbs'—anything from three to fifteen miles from the centre of London—and sometimes even further away. They come into London by bus, by tube (or Underground railway), by train or by car. Every day three million people are taken into and out of London by one or other of these. They are often called 'commuters', and a few come to work in London every day from places as far away as Birmingham and Bristol.

Olaf is going to travel by tube. The Underground station is only about four minutes' walk from where he lives. Crowds of other business men and girls, typists, secretaries, shop-assistants, etc., are hurrying into the station to get to their offices by nine o'clock or nine-thirty. In the station, some people are queueing for tickets at the ticket-office, but those who have the correct change use the automatic ticket machines. Olaf has a 'season ticket'[1] which he bought at the station yesterday, so he simply shows it to the ticket-collector at the barrier, steps on to the descending escalator[2] (or moving stairway), and in a short time is on the crowded platform watching the train come in (during 'rush hours'[3] there is a train to the City every minute). A quarter of an hour later sees him

---

[1] Instead of buying a ticket for each journey, you can buy a 'season ticket' for a week, a month, three months (a 'quarterly' ticket), six months (a 'half-yearly' ticket) or a year. With this you can make the journey as often as you wish without extra payment.

[2] A few older stations still have lifts.

[3] 'Rush hours' are from 8.0 to 9.30 a.m. and 4.30 to 6.30 p.m.

at Bank station (which is just by the Bank of England). He is quickly out of the train and on to the escalator again. A few minutes later he is out of the station and is in 'the City', one of the busiest centres of commerce in the world. In front of him is an imposing building which looks like a fortress, the Bank of England. Behind him is the Mansion House, the official residence of the Lord Mayor of London. Nearby is the Stock Exchange, and a short distance on his right is Lloyd's, the shipping insurance corporation. Further away on his left he can just see the golden cross of St. Paul's Cathedral. But Olaf has no time for sightseeing this morning. He walks quickly away from the station and within another five minutes he is at the office of the Weavewell Woollen Co. Ltd. in Victoria Street.

Exercises

I WORD STUDY. *Use the following:*

suburbs (and the adjective *suburban*), underground, tube (what is the other meaning?), commuter (use also *commute*; what is the meaning of 'to commute a prison sentence'?), typist (use also *to type*, *typewriter*), secretary, shop-assistant (use also *assist* and *assistance*), queue (note the pronunciation [kju:]), change (several meanings), barrier, escalator, platform, lift (in the U.S.A. a *lift* is called an *elevator*. Note the other meaning of *lift*), sightseeing.

II IDIOMS. *Explain and make other examples:*

1. *a great many* people; 2. they live *anything* from three to fifteen miles from London; 3. Olaf *has no time for* sightseeing (two meanings); 4. Olaf *is going to travel* by tube; 5. the station is *about four minutes' walk* from where he lives; 6. the *rush* hours; 7. *within another five minutes* he is walking into the office.

III *Answer the following:*

1. What is 'the City'? 2. Do the people who work in the City live there? Where do they usually live? What name is often

given to them? 3. How do they travel to the City? 4. Whom does Olaf see hurrying into the station? 5. What is a queue? 6. What is a 'season ticket'? 7. Where do you buy a railway ticket? 8. What is another word for the *Underground*? 9. How are you carried up and down at a tube station? 10. How often is there a train to the City during rush hours? 11. Where is 'Bank' station in London? 12. What is the American word for a *lift*?

3
How Olaf got his Job

export   import   merchant   commerce   routine   firm   trade
sales manager   department   correspondence   acknowledgment
interview   telephone   application

About the middle of September Olaf's father, an export and import merchant in Stockholm, had written to his son and asked him what his plans and ideas for the future were. Olaf had answered that he had not finally made up his mind. He had had two years in London and he thought he had put those two years to good use. He now had a fairly good knowledge of English and could understand and make himself understood in everyday conversation. He would, of course, like to go into his father's business one day; but it seemed to him that it would be most useful to him first to get a sound knowledge of English commercial practice, about which he knew so little. He remembered that his father had a number of business friends in London and wondered whether his father could, perhaps, give him one or two introductions.

Within a few days he had a reply from his father:

8, Kungsgatan,
Stockholm.
20th September, 19—.

My dear Olaf,

Many thanks for your letter, which arrived yesterday. We were all very pleased to hear that you are keeping well,

CHAPTER 3

and I was, of course, most interested in what you wrote.

You know that I had always hoped that you would come into the firm some day and I am very glad that you want to do this. I think that your suggestion that you should get some experience of commercial practice is excellent. *Practice* is the important thing. You can study Theory and Economics anywhere, but you can only learn the real day-to-day routine by actually working in an office; and probably nowhere better than in London, which is still an important centre of world trade.

Obviously, it would be a great advantage if you could get into a really modern and well-organised business house. Fortunately, I can give you an introduction to a firm which will, I think, give you exactly what you need. I have been doing business for many years with the Weavewell Woollen Co. Ltd., which, as the name tells you, is in the textile trade. They stand today in the front rank of London textile firms and have first class connections in the home and export trade.

I have known the Manager, Mr. Clifford, for many years, and their Sales Manager, Mr. Austin, was in Stockholm last spring when I gave him quite a good order. Both are extremely pleasant and efficient men and if you can get into that firm I am sure they will certainly try to help you as much as they can.

I enclose a copy of a letter I have sent today to Mr. Clifford and if you write to him and refer to my letter he will probably ask you to come and see him.

Let me know how you are getting on.

    We all send our love and best wishes.

FATHER

HOW OLAF GOT HIS JOB

This is the letter that Olaf's father sent to Mr. Clifford:

8, Kungsgatan,
Stockholm.
20th September, 19—.

E. Clifford, Esq.,
Weavewell Woollen Co. Ltd.,
Victoria Street,
London, EC4X 1SH[1]

Dear Mr. Clifford,

It is a long time since we last met, but I still remember the very pleasant evening we spent together at the Savoy[2] about five years ago. I believe I told you at the time that my son was growing up and that I was thinking of sending him to London for a few years. You know how important it is in a business like ours to have a full command of the English language. Well, Olaf has been in London for two years now and seems to have been extremely lucky with his teacher, a Mr. Priestley, so I think my son's English will be all right. But he has hardly any business experience at all, and that is the reason for this letter. Do you think it would be possible to take him into Weavewell's and to show him the actual work of a well-organised firm in all its departments? Please don't misunderstand me. I don't want him just to look on, to be a nuisance to you, and to get bored himself. I want him to gain practical experience by working in several departments and doing the various jobs himself.

I know I am asking a lot, but I should appreciate it very much if you could help me in this matter and so strengthen the friendly relations which have existed between our firms for so long.

---

[1] Most addresses include a postcode, which identifies the destination of a letter with great precision. The code makes it possible for the Post Office to sort letters entirely by machine.
[2] A big hotel in London.

I have sent a copy of this letter to my son, and he will probably write to you shortly.

With many thanks and kindest regards,

Yours very sincerely,

SVEN PETERSEN

'. . . a full command of the English language'

The same morning that Olaf got his father's letter he sat down and wrote to Mr. Clifford:

18, Ladbroke Terrace,
London, NW4Y 1HR
27th September, 19—.

E. Clifford, Esq.,
Weavewell Woollen Co. Ltd.,
Victoria Street,
London, EC4X 1SH

Dear Sir,

My father, Mr. Sven Petersen of Stockholm, has informed me that he has written to you and asked you whether it would be possible for me to work in your firm in order to gain some commercial experience. I am writing to you, therefore, to give you a few particulars about myself.

HOW OLAF GOT HIS JOB

I am 21 years of age and after leaving school I worked in my father's business for a short time. My business experience, however, is very limited; quite frankly, I know nothing about English commercial practice and correspondence, but am very anxious to learn all I can. As my father has told you, I came to England about two years ago and studied English with an excellent teacher, Mr. Priestley, and he says I now have quite a good knowledge of the language. In addition to Swedish and Norwegian I speak and write French and German fairly well, and a friend is teaching me Spanish.

If you could find me any position in your office, no matter how small the job was, I should be very much obliged, and you may be assured that I would spare no effort to fill it to your satisfaction.

Yours faithfully,

OLAF PETERSEN

'... a friend is teaching me Spanish'

Weavewell Woollen Co. Ltd.
Victoria Street,
London, EC4X ISH

GM/MS   3rd October, 19—.

O. Petersen, Esq.,
18, Ladbroke Terrace,
London, NW4Y IHR

Dear Sir,

    Our General Manager, Mr. Clifford, has asked me to acknowledge your letter of 27th September, regarding your application for a position in this firm. He would like to discuss the matter with you, and I am writing to ask you to come to this office for an interview on Wednesday, 14th October, at 3 p.m.

    If this time should not suit you I should be obliged if you would telephone me (173 7431)[1] in order to fix a convenient date.

                                   Yours faithfully,
                                   MARGARET SHARPE
                                   Secretary to Mr. Clifford

Exercises

I WORD STUDY. *Use the following:*

merchant (also *merchandise*), **business** (use also *busy*, *busily*), **introduction**, **delay**, **firm** (note several meanings), **suggestion** (use also *suggest*), **experience** (verb and noun), **commerce** (and *commercial*), **practice** (use also *practise*, *practical* and *practically*), **theory** (use also *theoretical*), **routine**, **actually**, **obviously**, **advantage** (what is the opposite?), **textile**, **efficient**, **enclose** (also *enclosure*), **refer** (also *reference*), **well-organised** (also

---

[1] Most towns in Britain now have all-figure telephone numbers. If Olaf were to telephone from outside the London area, he would first dial the London code, 01, and then all the numbers that Miss Sharpe has given.

organise, organisation), department, misunderstand, nuisance, bored, appreciate, job, shortly (meaning 'soon'; what is the meaning of 'he will write to you *briefly*'?), increase (verb and noun. What is the opposite?), inform (also *information*), limited (also *limit* and *unlimited*), frankly, anxious (what is the noun from this?), satisfaction (use also *satisfactory, satisfy, unsatisfactory*), acknowledge (use also *knowledge* and *acknowledgment*), discuss, interview, suit [sju:t] (also *suitable, unsuitable*. Note other meanings of *suit*. What is a *suite* [swi:t]?) convenient (use also *inconvenient* and *convenience*).

II IDIOMS. *Explain and use in sentences:*

1. he had not *made up his mind*; 2. he had *put* those years *to good use*; 3. *everyday conversation*; 4. I want to answer your letter *without delay*; 5. it would be *a great advantage*; 6. My son is *growing up*; 7. I am *thinking of* sending him to London; 8. I don't want him just *to look on*; 9. my business experience *is very limited*; 10. if you could find me a position *no matter how small* it was; 11. I would *spare no effort* to please you.

III 1. What is the difference between *export* and *import*? 2. Explain *the home and export trade*. 3. What is the textile trade? 4. Who is in charge of the sales in a business? 5. Why is a knowledge of English useful in business? 6. How did Olaf's father want him to gain practical experience? 7. What is the meaning of *Commercial Correspondence*? 8. What is meant by *acknowledging a letter*? 9. What is *an interview*?

IV *Write short letters:*

a) acknowledging a letter;
b) asking someone to come for an interview.

4
Olaf Writes to his Father

staff   salary   rise   offer   accept

18, Ladbroke Terrace,
London, NW4Y 1HR
15th October, 19—.

Dear Father,

    I am going to join the staff of Weavewell Woollen Company. Isn't that good news? I followed your suggestion and wrote to the Manager, Mr. Clifford, and yesterday I went, at his request, to an interview. I saw him and the Company Secretary, Mr. Smithson. They asked me a few questions—chiefly, I think, to test my knowledge of English—and I didn't do too badly. Mr. Clifford asked me what sort of job I had in mind, and I replied that, as I wanted to gain experience in business generally, I would accept any work which gave me a chance of learning the routine of office work. Well, to cut a long story short, Mr. Clifford said he thought the best way would be for me to start right from the bottom and work through the departments. He warned me that I might find the work dull and monotonous at first, but that there would be a good chance of promotion after the first six months if I showed that I was worth it. The salary would not be big, but here again he assured me that there would be a rise if I proved satisfactory. Of course, I accepted the offer and they said they would like me to make a start on October 19th.

    Thanks for helping me to get the job. I hope you are all well at home.

Much love and all good wishes,
OLAF

OLAF WRITES TO HIS FATHER

'... to cut a long story short'

Exercises

I WORD STUDY. *Use the following:*

staff, test (noun and verb), accept, warn (and *warning*), monotonous, promotion (also *promote*), salary (how does this differ from *wages*?), assure (use also *sure* and *insure*).

II IDIOMS. *Explain and use in sentences of your own:*

1. To *join the staff*. 2. I *followed your suggestion*. 3. I went *at his request*. 4. I *didn't do too badly*. 5. He asked me what sort of job I *had in mind*. 6. *To cut a long story short*. 7. I am going to *start from the bottom*. 8. There would be a *rise* if I *proved satisfactory*. 9. I am going to *make a start* on Monday. 10. There would be promotion *if I was worth it*.

III *Answer the following:*

1. What is the purpose of an interview? 2. Give a word meaning 'all the people who work for a firm'. 3. What position had Mr. Smithson in the firm? 4. What was Mr. Clifford? 5. When would Olaf get promotion if he was worth it? 6. What warning did Mr. Clifford give Olaf? 7. Where was Olaf going to start? 8. What was he going to do after that? 9. What kind of salary was he going to get? 10. When was Olaf going to make a start?

IV *Write a short letter to a friend saying that you have just got a job and telling him a little about it.*

5
Confirming an Appointment

confirm   appointment

The day after his interview Olaf received the following letter:

Weavewell Woollen Co. Ltd.
Victoria Street,
London, EC4X 1SH

GM/MS 14th October, 19—.
O. Petersen, Esq.,
18, Ladbroke Terrace,
London, NW4Y 1HR

Dear Mr. Petersen,

I have pleasure in confirming our conversation of today. As agreed, you will begin work on 19th October at a salary of £15 per week. Our office hours are from 9.30 a.m. to 5.30 p.m., with one hour for lunch, and every other Saturday from 9.30 a.m. to 12.30. p.m.

If you will come and see me on Monday when you arrive at the office, I will introduce you to Mr. Brown, under whom you will work at first.

Yours sincerely,
p.p.[1] Weavewell Woollen Co. Ltd.
E. CLIFFORD
Manager

---

[1] See p. 50 (footnote).

CONFIRMING AN APPOINTMENT

To this he replied:

18, Ladbroke Terrace,
London, NW4Y 1HR
15th October, 19—.

E. Clifford, Esq.,
Weavewell Woollen Co. Ltd.,
Victoria Street,
London, EC4X 1SH

Dear Sir,
Your Ref. GM/MS
I thank you for your letter of 14th October and am writing to confirm that I agree to it in every respect. I am grateful to you and Mr. Smithson for giving me this opportunity and shall endeavour to do all I can to justify your confidence.

Yours faithfully,
OLAF PETERSEN

Exercises

I WORD STUDY. *Use the following:*

confirm (also *confirmation*), appointment, pleasure (use also *please, pleasant, unpleasant, displeased*), grateful (also *gratitude, ungrateful, ingratitude*), opportunity, endeavour, justify, confidence (also *confident, confidently*).

II IDIOMS. *Explain and use in sentences of your own:*
1. *As agreed*, you will begin work on 19th October. 2. Your salary will be £15 *per week*. 3. You will work *every other Saturday* morning. 4. I agree *in every respect*.

III *Write short letters:*
a) confirming an appointment offered at an interview;
b) acknowledging the confirmation and accepting the appointment.

6
The Manager's Room

desk   'in-tray'   'out-tray'   waste-paper basket   envelope
fountain pen   pencil   paper-clip   elastic bands   file
earphone   keys   dictate   'dictaphone'

Mr. Clifford had told Olaf to report to him on his arrival, so he made his way up to the third floor where the manager's room was, and knocked at the door. 'Come in,' said a voice on the other side, and Olaf entered. 'Ah! Good morning, Mr. Petersen. I'm glad to see you. Take a seat. Will you just excuse me a moment while I look through the rest of these letters?' Olaf sat down and looked round the room. Mr. Clifford was sitting at a large desk on which was a telephone, an 'in-tray' for incoming letters and an 'out-tray' for letters to go to the post, and by his side was a waste-paper basket into which he dropped the envelopes from the letters that he had opened. There was an ashtray on his left and on his right were two or three pencils, a fountain pen and a small box of paper-clips,[1] elastic bands for holding together papers and two or three files[2] containing papers that he was going to examine.

In a corner of his room, at a smaller desk, sat Miss Sharpe, his secretary, busily typing some letters which Mr. Clifford had previously recorded for her on his dictating machine, or 'dictaphone'.[3] Olaf watched her fingers moving rapidly over the keys, then saw her pause for a moment, listening to the tape in the machine, which she controlled with a pedal under

---

[1] Or *paper-fasteners*.

[2] *file* here = box or paper folder in which documents, letters, etc., are kept in order. Look up other meanings in your dictionary.

[3] As Mr. Clifford reads the morning's letters he speaks the answers into the machine; they are recorded and can be played back later and typed by his secretary.

her desk. A thin wire led to a very small earphone plugged into Miss Sharpe's ear, so Olaf could hear nothing except the sound of her typewriter. He saw her take out the typed sheet, put another one in, and then quickly start on that page.

'Well, Mr. Petersen, I'm ready now,' said Mr. Clifford. 'Come along, we'll go and see Mr. Brown, our office manager, who will be your boss[4] for the next month or so.'

Exercises

I WORD STUDY. *Use the following:*

report (verb and noun), excuse (noun and verb. Note the difference in pronunciation [iks'kjuːs] [iks'kjuːz]), telephone, ashtray, waste-paper basket, elastic band, fountain pen, typist (also *to type* and *typewriter*), keys (two meanings), boss, sheet (two meanings), tape, control (verb and noun), pedal, wire, plug (verb and noun).

II IDIOMS. *Explain and use in sentences of your own:*

1. He *made his way* up to *the third floor*. 2. *Take a seat*. 3. Excuse me a moment while I *look through* these letters. (Compare: 'Olaf *looked round* the room.') 4. The files contained papers that *he was going to examine*. 5. She *took out* one sheet and *put in* another. 6. He will be your boss *for the next month or so*.

III *Answer the following:*

1. Where was Mr. Clifford's room? 2. What was Mr. Clifford doing when Olaf entered? 3. Mention the things on Mr. Clifford's desk. 4. What is an 'in-tray'? 5. What is put into an 'out-tray'? 6. Into what did Mr. Clifford drop the envelopes from the letters he opened? 7. What are (a) paper-clips, (b) elastic bands, used for? 8. What is a *file*? 9. Where was Miss Sharpe sitting? 10. What was she doing? 11. What is a *dictating machine*? 12. What position had Mr. Brown?

IV *Write a short description of the manager's office.*

---

[4]*boss* [bɔs] = master; person in charge (*colloquial*).

7
The General Office

system   sample   date stamp   tray   sales   buyer
price list   catalogue   inquiry[1]   warehouse   delivery order
advice note   accounts   cheque   statement   solicitors
Inland Revenue   advertisement   mail   assess   tax
distribute

The main office into which Mr. Clifford took Olaf was a large well-lighted room, pleasantly warm from the central heating, but kept fresh by 'air-conditioning'. There were twelve or thirteen clerks at work, each at his own desk, and at a larger desk sat Mr. Brown, the Office Manager.

'Good morning, George,' said Mr. Clifford. (Mr. Clifford was very friendly with Mr. Brown.) 'This is the new man, Mr. Petersen, that I spoke to you about. He knows nothing at all about business yet, but he will go through a number of the departments to get a good knowledge of at least the general aspects of business life. Let him see as much as you can of the work of your department, show him how to write a business letter, explain the mysteries of the filing system—but I don't need to tell you what to do. You know, don't you, George?'

'Yes, Mr. Clifford, I quite understand. I'll look after Mr. Petersen.'

'Good. And how's the family? All well?'

'Yes, thanks.'

'That's fine. Well, goodbye for the present, Mr. Petersen. I'll leave you with Mr. Brown now.'

'Thank you, sir,' said Olaf. 'And I'll try to become a good business man.'

[1] *inquiry* or *enquiry*; both are correct.

THE GENERAL OFFICE

'Splendid,' said Mr. Clifford, smiling as he went out.

'And now, Mr. Petersen,' said Mr. Brown, 'let's get to work. The post has just been delivered. I want you to open the letters and help me to sort them. There's a date stamp on that desk. Stamp each letter when you take it out of the envelope. Make sure you don't leave anything in the envelopes.'

So Olaf cut them open, one after the other, stamped each letter with the date stamp and passed the letters to Mr. Brown, who quickly glanced at them. In front of him were a number of wire trays. One was marked 'Sales'. Into this he threw orders for goods or inquiries about goods. Another was marked 'Buyer'. Into that went price lists and catalogues and samples. Into the tray marked 'Warehouse' he threw delivery orders and advice notes. Into the 'Accounts' tray went cheques and statements of accounts.

'Oh, Mr. Brown, there's a cheque with this letter.'

'Yes, pin that to the letter or fasten it with a paper-clip so that it won't get lost.'

There was a letter from the firm's solicitors and one from the Inland Revenue[1] saying that the Inspector of Taxes was calling to see the Secretary. Those went into the tray marked 'Secretary'. Finally there were about half-a-dozen letters in reply to an advertisement for a typist that Mr. Brown had put in *The Times*. They went into the 'Office' tray.

'We'll work at those together later, Petersen,' said Mr. Brown. 'I want to get the mail distributed as quickly as possible. You can come with me as I take round these letters. Bring the trays and I'll introduce you to the head of each department.'

. . . . .

'Ah, well,' said Mr. Brown when they got back to the office. 'You've met all the heads of departments now. You'll spend

---

[1] *The Inland Revenue* is the Government Department concerned with assessing and collecting taxes, especially Income Tax.

some time with each of them later and get to know the work done in their department. Now let's get some of our office work done.'

Exercises

I WORD STUDY. *Use the following:*

well-lighted (or *well-lit*. Give the opposite), central heating, air-conditioning, dictate (also *dictation*), aspect, mystery ['mistəri] (also *mysterious* [mis'tiəriəs]), system (also *systematic*), post (several meanings. Use also *postman, postage, post office, postcard*), deliver (and *delivery*), sort (as a verb), stamp (noun and verb), envelope, glance (noun and verb), tray, catalogue, sample, warehouse, cheque (compare with *check*), account (use also *accountant*), solicitor, revenue, call (several meanings: here 'visit', in U.S.A. often 'telephone'), advertisement (use also *advertise*), mail, distribute [dis'tribjuːt] (use also *distribution* [distri'bjuːʃn]), assess (use *assessment*), tax (also *taxation*).

II IDIOMS. *Explain and use in sentences:*

1. Air-conditioning *kept it fresh*. 2. I'll *look after* Mr. Petersen. 3. How's the family? *All well? That's fine*. 4. Goodbye *for the present*. 5. Let's *get to work*. 6. *Make sure* you don't leave anything in the envelopes. 7. I'll *take round* the letters. 8. *You'll get to know* the work done there. 9. *Let's get* some of our office work *done*.

III *Answer the following:*

1. What kind of a room was the office? 2. How was it heated? 3. How was it kept fresh? 4. What kind of desk had Mr. Brown? 5. What was Mr. Brown doing when Olaf entered? 6. What was Olaf's first job in the office? 7. Describe exactly what he did. 8. How were the trays marked? 9. What did Mr. Brown put into the tray marked 'Sales'; what into the one marked 'Buyer'? 10. Where did he put samples and catalogues; where delivery orders and advice notes? 11. What did Olaf do with the cheque? 12. What are solicitors? 13. What does the Inland Revenue do? 14. Into which tray did Mr. Brown put

the replies to his advertisement? 15. Why is the incoming mail marked with a date stamp? 16. What do you do with enclosures when you are sorting the mail? 17. Why should letters be distributed as quickly as possible? 18. To which departments do these go: (a) price lists, (b) orders, (c) inquiries, (d) cheques?

8
Filing

**filing cabinet   customer   supplier   index   premises   repairs
shareholder   auditor   Income Tax   address   traveller   terms
mailing list   retail   office boy   tab   department stores
chain stores   wholesale   director   document**

MR. BROWN: Oh, Miss Carson, are you sorting out letters?

MISS CARSON: Yes, Mr. Brown.

MR. BROWN: Well, Mr. Petersen here will give you a hand with them. He doesn't know anything about filing yet, so will you take charge of him and explain the work to him?

(*Mr. Brown goes out*)

MISS CARSON: Certainly, Mr. Brown. Good morning, Mr. Petersen. Well, these are filing cabinets. The system is really quite simple, though it looks a little complicated at first. You see, every regular customer and every supplier of the firm has a file like this (*and she pulled out a file marked 'Lloyd & Baker'*), and every file goes in its appropriate cabinet in alphabetical order.

OLAF: But there are a lot of files, aren't there?

MISS CARSON: Oh yes, hundreds. Weavewell is a big firm, you know.

OLAF: But how do you know where to find the particular file that you want?

MISS CARSON: Well, you see, we have this index. In that, there is a card for every file.

OLAF: There are three colours of cards, I see; some are white, some are green and some are yellow. Why is that?

MISS CARSON: The green cards are for *customers*, that is firms who buy from us. The white cards are for *suppliers*, that is people who send us goods. The yellow ones are for *General* —oh, just anything that isn't 'Customer' or 'Supplier', like 'Landlord', 'Premises', 'Repairs', 'Shareholders', 'Auditors', 'Income Tax', etc. And then I keep a file for things that don't fall into any particular category and that may be needed later on. I call it 'Useful Information', and it has often proved very useful indeed.

OLAF: And I see some of the files are green, others white and others yellow. I suppose that is so that you can see that a 'customer's' file doesn't get put by mistake among the 'suppliers' or 'general'.

MISS CARSON: Exactly. If someone makes a mistake like that we can see it at once.

OLAF: May I have a look at one of the index cards?

MISS CARSON: Certainly. Here's one for example. You see it has the name and address of the firm on it, 'Lloyd & Baker, High St., Minehead.' Then there's the name of their buyer, 'R. Thompson'. Here's a note of the dates of our traveller's

OUT	DEPT.	INQ.	DIRECT ORDERS	TRAVS. VISIT	TRAVS. ORDERS	REMARKS.
16/6/71	S/M	14/9/71	£6.50	14/2/72	£38	
31/11/71 19/3/72	S/M S/M	2/4/72	—	26/8/72	—	Too late
14/7/72 3/12/73	S/M A/C	11/7/72	£12	14/1/73	£67	
16/2/73 20/7/73	S/M Man.			2/8/73	£94	
25/7/73 3/8/73	S/M A/C			3/2/74	£136	
				13/7/74		Overstocked
Always interested in bargain offers						Branches in Dunster and Porlock
30/2½, 60 net. Credit Limit £150						
High Street. Area: S/W. Traveller: R.A.Smith. Buyer: R. Thompson.						
LLOYD & BAKER. MINEHEAD						

Index Card

visits to Lloyd & Baker and the orders received—rather small ones—and this is the arrangement we have with them about terms.

OLAF: That's very useful.

MISS CARSON: Yes, it is. The index serves, too, as a mailing list.

OLAF: And what is a mailing list?

MISS CARSON: Oh, of course, I must explain. Well, a mailing list is a list of all firms to whom we may want to send some information or other. But things that interest one type of firm might not interest another, and that is the reason why we classify our index under various headings.

OLAF: Can you give me a few examples and tell me how you do it?

MISS CARSON: Well, let's take the customers' cards first. You see these square tabs on the right-hand side, and do you notice that they have five different colours? The white ones are for retail shops, the orange ones for department stores, the green ones for chain stores, blue is for exporters and yellow for small wholesalers. And the cards for suppliers are marked according to the articles and qualities they manufacture, woollen, cotton, rayon, silk, nylon, etc.

OLAF: That is clever, I must say.

MISS CARSON: Yes, we find it helpful. Why, only last week we sent out our new price list to all retail customers. And we just took the necessary information from the cards. Just excuse me a moment, there's my phone.

(*In a moment or two she is back again.*) That was Mr. Austin, our Sales Manager, on the phone. He wants the file for Hardman & Noel, Birmingham, and is sending the office boy for it. Here it is.

(*To the office boy who has just entered.*) Hello, Jones, you want the Hardman & Noel file for Mr. Austin, don't you?

JONES: Yes, Miss Carson. And he's sent back these two files that he had out yesterday.

FILING

MISS CARSON: Good. Just wait a moment. (*Olaf saw her take out the card marked 'Hardman & Noel, Birmingham'. She wrote on it the date 19/10/73 and S/M (Sales Manager). Then, before she put back the card, she marked it with a red tab; then she handed the file to the office boy.*)

MISS CARSON: There you are, Jones.

JONES: Thank you, miss (*and away he went with the file*).

OLAF: What's the idea of the red tab?

MISS CARSON: That's to mark an 'out' file. As you see, there are a number of cards marked like that including those for the two files that Jones has just returned. I want to deal with those now. What's the first one?

OLAF: 'Horrocks & Coates'. And the other one is 'Brownlow Wright'.

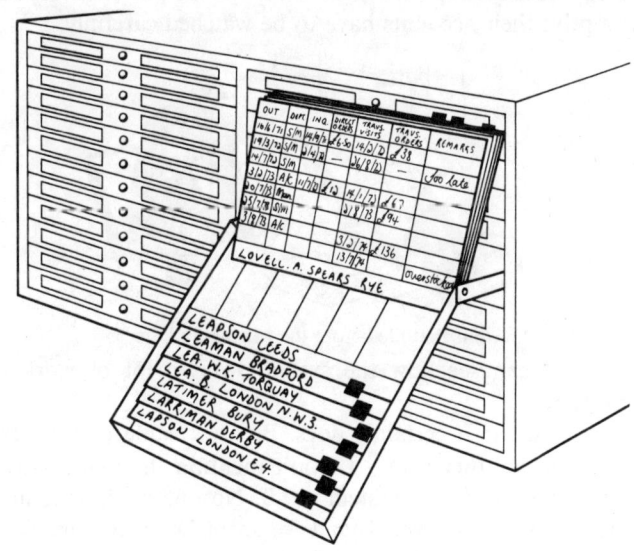

Classified visible index

MISS CARSON: Yes. Here are the cards, each with its red tab on. I've taken off the red tabs now and crossed through the dates because the files have been returned, and you can put the files in their right places.

OLAF: Certainly. This is the correct place, isn't it?

MISS CARSON: That's right.

OLAF: I see some of the cards have other coloured tabs on them. Why is that?

MISS CARSON: Oh, for various things. You can give a lot of information by different colours, sizes, and shapes of the tabs, and by their position on the card. This one, for example, is to remind me to put that file before the Managing Director on 22nd October. Those with green tabs have to go to the General Secretary on 1st November, and so on. And those few black ones are our 'black sheep', the people who don't pay their accounts promptly; their accounts have to be watched carefully.

'... put that file before the Managing Director'

OLAF: I can see how the system saves a lot of work and confusion.

MISS CARSON: It certainly does. Before I came to Weavewell I was with another firm—I won't mention the name—where there seemed to be no system at all. No one could ever find a thing when it was wanted, and we spent hours looking for it, whereas here we can find any letter or document in a moment. Oh yes, having a system certainly makes things easier.

Exercises

I WORD STUDY. *Use the following:*

cabinet, complicated, appropriate, alphabetical, particular (also *particulars*), landlord (use also *landlady* and *tenant*), category, mistake, retail (also *retailer*, giving the opposites), necessary, information (also *inform*), phone (short for *telephone*), include (can you give the opposite?), to cross out, classify (also *class*, *classification*), silk, rayon, various (use also *vary*, *variety*, *variable*, *invariably*), prompt (and *promptly*), size, confuse (and *confusion*), whereas.

II IDIOMS. *Explain and use:*

1. Mr. Petersen will *give you a hand* with the letters. 2. Will you *take charge* of him? 3. The file was put there *by mistake*. 4. The index *serves as* a mailing list. 5. The Sales Manager was *on the phone*. 6. That is clever, *I must say*. 7. *Why, only last week*, we sent out our new price list. 8. *What's the idea of* the red tab?

III 1. What is a filing cabinet? 2. Arrange these in alphabetical order: G, P, D, B, Y, S, L, E. 3. What was in the index? 4. Name the three main divisions into which the correspondence is sorted. 5. What is (a) a customer, (b) a supplier? 6. What are 'business premises'? 7. How is the correspondence of each firm kept together? 8. How can you tell which are customers' files and which are suppliers' files? 9. Where are the files kept? In what order? 10. How do you keep control of the files? 11. What is the use of tabs? 12. What would you expect to find in the 'General' file? 13. What information do you put on the index card? 14. What is a mailing list? 15. Can you give reasons why a mailing list is important? 16. Describe what is done when files are taken away and returned. 17. Explain the need for systematic filing.

9
The Office Equipment

typewriter   notebook   shorthand   stationery   postcard   memorandum   carbon paper   flimsy   draft   window-envelopes   letter-heading   continuation sheet   'inter-com'[1]   ribbon   circular   stencil   duplicating machine   telex   addressing machine

For the moment Olaf has no work on hand and he glances round the department. 'It certainly is a beehive of activity,' he thinks. Ten typists are working at their electric typewriters; most are wearing earphones and are typing from the dictating machines beside them, which they stop and start with foot controls. One girl is typing from a shorthand notebook beside her typewriter, and hardly ever looks at the keyboard. On each desk is a shelf with several trays in which the necessary stationery is kept. There are sheets of notepaper with Weavewell's letter-heading, small memorandum forms, postcards, carbon paper and flimsy paper for copies, sheets of paper without the firm's letter-heading for drafts and documents, envelopes in various sizes (Weavewell's use window-envelopes where possible), continuation sheets for letters which need several pages, etc. Now and then the telephone rings, or the managing director speaks on the 'inter-com' to the senior typist who works as his 'private secretary'.

Olaf walks over to a typist who is putting a strange-looking sheet into her machine. She is preparing a 'circular' by typing a 'stencil'. This is a waxed sheet which is typed in the same way as an ordinary letter but still more carefully. The stencil

---

[1] *'inter-com'* = intercommunication, i.e. internal telephone system of the office, providing connections between all the different departments.

is fixed on to one of Weavewell's three different types of duplicating machines, and Olaf watches with great interest as, in a few minutes, several hundreds of clear and clean copies are produced which look almost exactly the same as a typewritten letter. The different machines have different advantages and disadvantages, and which machine is used on a particular occasion depends on the number and quality of the copies required, as well as on the type of material to be copied.

'... putting a strange-looking sheet into her machine'

Against the wall is an impressive-looking machine which Olaf guesses must be the Telex.[1] This has a keyboard like that of a typewriter, and printed messages can be transmitted direct to other firms which have the system, whether at home or overseas. It is by far the quickest and most accurate method of communication with customers abroad, and Weavewell's foreign trade has certainly 'speeded up' since they had the system installed.

There is another smaller but very useful machine which Olaf had never seen before: the addressing machine. The addresses of the various firms are typed on small stencils which are arranged in special trays sorted into convenient categories.

[1] Or teleprinter.

When, for example, the Accounts Department wants a statement for practically every regular customer at the end of the month, the customers' stencils are 'fed' into the machine and many hundreds of statements are addressed with very little time and trouble.

Notes

The standard paper for letters and publications is known as *A4*, and measures 210 mm × 297 mm (8·3″ × 11·7″). Many firms, however, still use *octavo* (125 mm × 200 mm = 5″ × 8″), *quarto* (200 mm × 250 mm = 8″ × 10″) or *foolscap* (200 mm × 320 mm = 8″ × 12·75″) paper.

A *memorandum* (*memo*), plural *memoranda*, is a note made to keep something in mind, a short record of events or of a conversation, etc.

Carbon paper is thin paper covered with a black substance. It is placed between two sheets of writing paper and produces on the lower one a copy of what is written or typed on that above.

Flimsy is very thin paper on which carbon copies are taken.

Draft here means a rough plan of a scheme or document (for other meanings see pages 203-4).

A *window-envelope* is an envelope with a transparent piece in front through which the name and address written or typed on the letter inside can be read. This saves the typist the trouble of typing the name and address again on the envelope and prevents mistakes.

A *circular* is a document, usually a notice or an advertisement written in the form of a letter. Many copies are made at the same time and sent to a number of people.

Exercises

I WORD STUDY. *Use the following:*

glance (noun and verb), bee (and *beehive*), activity [æk'tiviti] (also *active* ['æktiv], *action, activities, inactive*), shorthand, shelf

THE OFFICE EQUIPMENT

(what is the plural? Give three other words that form their plural in the same way), connect (also *connection, disconnect*), wax, machine (and *machinery*), memory (use also *remember*), substance, lower (adj. What is the opposite?), scheme (note the pronunciation [ski:m]), transparent, prevent, install (and *installed, installation*).

II IDIOMS. *Explain and use:*

1. *Now and then* the telephone rings. 2. A memorandum is a note made *to keep something in mind*. 3. This *saves her the trouble* of typing it again. 4. Business has *speeded up* in the last few weeks. 5. They *had the machine installed*.

III *Put in the missing prepositions or adverbs:*

1. Olaf glanced —— the department.
2. She hardly ever looks —— the keyboard.
3. A senior typist works as Private Secretary —— the Managing Director.
4. He speaks —— her —— the 'inter-com'.
5. It provides a connection —— all departments —— the firm.
6. She works —— his private secretary.
7. The addresses —— the firms are typed —— stencils which are arranged —— trays.
8. The Accounts Department wants a statement —— every customer —— the end —— the month.
9. Carbon paper is thin paper covered —— a black substance. It is placed —— two sheets —— writing paper.

IV *Do the following:*

1. On page 34 we show the standard keyboard of an English typewriter. Compare it with your machine and say whether or where it is different.
2. How many types of stationery can you remember? What are the standard sizes of paper used for letters, etc.?
3. Explain fully how to make a carbon copy.
4. What are 'window-envelopes'? What are the advantages of using them?

5. For what purpose in your office would you use: (a) foolscap paper, (b) memorandum forms?
6. Why is flimsy paper used for copies?
7. What do you take for the second and third page of a letter?
8. What instrument besides the telephone is used for communication between departments?
9. Give an example of when you might use a circular.
10. What is a stencil? How is it prepared?
11. Describe any methods of duplicating you know.
12. What is an addressing machine and how does it work?

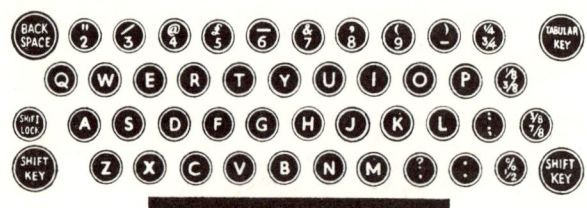

Typewriter Keyboard

10
The Telephone[1] Switchboard

**earphones   switchboard   exchange   telephonist   operator
extension   plug   dial   trunk   invoice   cable   directory**

Separated from the main room is the office telephone switchboard. Here Miss Clarke sits with earphones over her head and works the many extensions on the switchboard. Every department has at least one telephone; most of them have several. In the general office, for example, there is one for Mr. Brown, one for the Director's secretary, one for typists and one for the filing clerk. Each extension has a 'house number'—Mr. Brown is number 14, Mr. Clifford is 27—and the list of numbers hangs right in front of Miss Clarke. Olaf stood and watched her taking incoming calls and plugging them through to the department

Telephone Switchboard

[1] There is only one telephone system in Great Britain. It is a national one and is run by the Post Office.

that was wanted, or putting calls through to exchanges in London or to more distant exchanges. Olaf was impressed by her politeness; she answered every incoming call with a cheerful 'Weavewell's. Good morning', which gave a friendly start to even the most formal telephone call. He stood listening.

'... I'll put you through when he is free'

'Is that Mr. Brown? Mr. Austin to speak to you. ... Is that Ilford 2408?[1] Just a moment, please. You're through now to Ilford, Mr. Hammond. ... You want Mr. Clifford? Who's that speaking, please? Just hold on a moment; he's speaking on the other line. I'll put you through when he's free. ... Are you there,

---

[1] Although most telephone numbers in Britain are now all-figure, the name of the town or exchange is used when answering the phone or when looking for a number in the telephone directory. So if Miss Clarke wishes to telephone somebody in the Sheffield area, she will find his number in the Sheffield directory, then find the Sheffield code in the dialling code booklet. She will dial, say, 0742 23840, and the person answering the phone will probably say 'Sheffield 23840'. (Weavewell's keep telephone directories of some of the most important commercial centres in the country, as well as those covering the 'Greater London' area.)

I am putting you through now. . . . Mr. Austin? I'm sorry, his number is engaged at the moment. Can I ring you back in a few minutes. Town 2148, very well, thank you. . . .

You want Northwood 52934? Just a moment, please.' As Northwood is not a London exchange[1] she dials its code number (09274) followed by the given number. 'Is that Northwood five two nine three four? . . . Just a moment; I have a call for you. You're through to Northwood now, Miss Carson. . . . What was the number please, Mr. Clifford? Dunvegan 2255. Right! I'll ring you when I get through.' She dials 100. 'Operator, this is Town 7431. I want Dunvegan, 2255—no, double five' (and she pronounces it 'fife'), 'that's right. . . . Is that Dunvegan double two double five? Just a moment. Your Dunvegan number is on the line now, Mr. Clifford. . . .' Jones hands her a telegram, she glances at it and dials the code for telegrams. 'Is that telegrams? This is Town 7431. I have a telegram for Hardman. H for Harry, A for Andrew, R for Robert, D for David, M for Mary, A for Andrew, N for Nellie. And the address is Morton Street. M for Mary, O for Oliver,[2] R for Robert, T for Tommy, O for Oliver, N for Nellie. Morton Street, Kineton. K for King, I for Isaac, N for Nellie, E for Edward, T for Tommy, O for Oliver, N for Nellie. Here's the message:

> Goods sent today. Invoice following.
> Weavewells.

Will you repeat the message, please. . . . That's right. Thank you. Goodbye.'

OLAF (*as the calls stop for a moment*): Miss Clarke, why did you have to dial 100 and ask the operator to connect you to the number in Dunvegan?

---

[1] Within a 12–mile radius from Oxford Circus.
[2] Sometimes 'O for Orange'. The other words used for spelling a telegram, cable, etc., are B for Benjamin, C for Charlie, F for Frederick, G for George, J for Jack, L for Lucy, P for Peter, Q for Queenie, S for Sugar, U for Uncle, V for Victory, W for William, X for X-ray, Y for Yellow, Z for Zebra.

MISS CLARKE: That was because the exchange at Dunvegan isn't fully automatic yet, so you can't dial it direct.

OLAF: I see. One other question—what do you do when you want to find somebody's telephone number, but don't have the directory for the area in which he lives?

MISS CLARKE: Well, we keep quite a number of directories here, and of course we have our own list of numbers that we need regularly. But if I can't find a number myself, I simply dial the code (shown in the 'Dialling Instructions' booklet) for 'Directory Enquiries', and they very quickly give me the information I want. You can find out the time, or the weather forecast, or get motoring information and even cooking recipes, just by dialling the appropriate codes. Oh, and don't forget, if you ever find yourself in trouble and need the police, an ambulance or the fire brigade, you must dial 999 and ask for whichever emergency service you need.[1]

OLAF: I certainly hope I shall never have to make an emergency call—and I hope I shall never have to look after the telephone switchboard; I should be quite lost with all those plugs and switches. I think it's marvellous the way you manage, Miss Clarke.

MISS CLARKE: Oh, it's quite simple when you are used to it. . . . 'Weavewell's. Good morning.'

Exercises

I WORD STUDY. *Use the following:*

separate (verb and adjective. Note the difference in pronunciation ['sepəreit] and ['seprit]), impress (also *impression*), polite (use also *politeness*, *politely*), formal (use also *informal*, *formality*), double, telegram (use also *telegraph*), emergency, message (and *messenger*), marvel (noun and verb; use also

[1] Two further services are the 'personal call', whereby for an additional charge you can make absolutely sure of speaking only to the person you want; and 'transferred charge' call, for which the person to whom you are telephoning will pay—provided that he agrees to accept the call.

marvellous, marvellously), switch (noun and verb), cable (noun and verb; use also *cablegram*, telephonist [ti′lefənist]), forecast (noun and verb), ambulance.

II *Mark where the accent falls on each of the following words. Use each in a sentence:*

commerce, commercial; distribute, distribution; vary, variety; imports, imported; inform, information; invite, invitation.

III *Answer the following:*

1. What is the centre of the telephone system of a firm? 2. Describe a switchboard. 3. What is an extension? 4. What does the telephonist wear over her head? 5. Give some of the phrases used by the telephonist. 6. How do you (a) call the operator, (b) get a number that you don't know? 7. How would you send a telegram by phone? 8. What number would you dial in an emergency? 9. How would you spell MEXICO and SWEDEN on the telephone? 10. How would you say these numbers on the telephone: 0137, 4451, 6733, 7200, 5885, 2000? (The answer to this is at the foot of this page. Don't cheat!)

Answers to Question 10
oh one three seven; double four five one; six seven double three; seven two double oh; five eight eight five; two thousand.

11
The Work of the General Office

**apprentice   executive   organisation   signature book
blotting-paper   mailing clerk   registered post   air mail
Post Office Guide   enclosure (to enclose)   'sticker'
postage rate**

From his desk facing the big room Mr. Brown keeps an eye on everything that is going on in the department, and Olaf has the feeling that he is keeping an eye on him, too, though in a very quiet and friendly way. Now and then he exchanges a few words with him, and Olaf soon notices that Mr. Brown's work is not limited to the general office only. Together with Mr. Clifford he is responsible for the smooth working of the various departments, for stationery and equipment, for the necessary repairs and for an even distribution of the work. When, for example, the warehouse is very busy, he may lend them an office boy or one of the apprentices; he helps, if necessary, the Invoice Department or the Accounts Department by taking a typist off a less urgent job and sending her over to that department.

'Flexibility is the essence of organisation,' he likes to say; 'if you work in watertight compartments you'll never get anywhere.' He has the welfare of the staff at heart (he has engaged most of them himself and therefore takes a fatherly interest in them), he listens to and tries to smooth out their little troubles and complaints.

An hour or two before the office closes the typists and secretaries take their letters with the copies to the executives[1] who dictated them, to have them signed.[2] For this purpose a *Signa-*

---
[1] An executive member of the firm is one who has the authority to make important decisions for the firm.

[2] Some firms use a cheque-signing machine which reproduces the executive's signature, but Weavewell's have decided not to adopt this system.

THE WORK OF THE GENERAL OFFICE

'... we don't work in watertight compartments'

ture Book is used which consists of sheets of thick blotting-paper. The letters are placed between these sheets, and the Director or Manager is thus saved the trouble of blotting every single signature. But he reads the letters very carefully and every correction he makes in a letter is marked on the copy too. Then he checks whether the necessary enclosures are attached. In Weavewell's a system of numbered 'stickers' is used. One is stuck to the bottom corner of the letter and one with the same number is attached to the enclosure. All the mailing clerk has to do is to make sure that the two numbers agree. (If there are several enclosures in one letter, then two, three or more stickers will be fixed to it and the clerk has to look out for the various papers with the same numbers.) The letters are passed to the mailing clerk, whose job has become a little less tedious since Mr. Brown had a letter-folding machine installed in the department. The clerk puts the letters into their envelopes, and then feeds them into a franking machine which prints stamps on the envelopes at astonishing speed. (This machine has a meter which records the cost of the postage as it is printed, and Weavewell's pay the Post Office quarterly.) Documents and other important papers are sent 'Registered' or by 'Recorded Delivery' and a Post Office receipt is obtained for them. Most letters overseas are sent 'Air Mail' and stamped accordingly, but all letters to Europe now go by air at the ordinary rate. The mailing clerk is responsible for correct stamping and in case of doubt he looks it up in the official 'Post Office Guide' which is on sale at every Post Office.

Most firms with a big mailing department keep a copy of the Post Office Guide because it contains a lot of useful information, e.g. a summary of all the services offered by the Post Office, including savings schemes and the National Giro service; the postage rates for letters, postcards, printed papers and parcels in the United Kingdom[1] and to foreign countries; the registration fees for registering letters and parcels in Britain and the insurance fees for insuring mail going overseas; the charges for sending money through the post either by postal order or money order; the fees for the telephone, telegraph and telex services. It explains the system of the Business Reply Service[2] and gives information about details and frequency of postal services all over the world. The mailing clerk has to refer to this book almost daily and it is his responsibility to keep it up to date by marking in it the many changes which are constantly taking place.

All letters and postcards for Europe are sent by the quickest route (generally by air) without additional charge. With these air mail labels should not be used. For other countries, e.g.

---

[1] The United Kingdom consists of Great Britain (England, Scotland and Wales) and Northern Ireland. For convenience, 'Great Britain' or 'Britain' are sometimes used instead of 'The United Kingdom'.

[2] This service enables a business man to prepay the postage on the reply (letter or postcard) which he wants from his customer.

U.S.A., countries of South America, the cost for air mail varies.

Special Air Letter forms are on sale at the Post Office; the postage on these is less than on ordinary air mail letters.

Exercises

I WORD STUDY. *Use the following:*

limit (noun and verb. Use also *limited* and *unlimited*), responsible (use also *responsibility* and *irresponsible*), smooth (adj. and verb), even (note two or more meanings. What are the first three *even numbers*?), distribution [distri'bju:ʃn] (use also *distribute* [dis'tribju:t]), urgent, equipment (use also *equip*), flexible (use also *flexibility*), essence (use also *essential*), organise (also *organiser, organisation*), watertight (note also *airtight*), compartment, welfare (how does this differ from *farewell*?), complain (also *complaint*), signature (what is the corresponding verb?), fold (noun and verb), receipt (note the pronunciation [ri'si:t]. What is the corresponding verb?), ordinary (what is the opposite?), check (compare with *cheque*), attach (the opposite is *detach*. Note the pronunciation of these words [ə'tætʃ], [di'tætʃ]), stick (verb. Give the principal parts), agree (use also *agreement, agreeable*. Give the opposite of each of these), add (also *addition, additional*).

II IDIOMS AND PHRASES. *Use each of the following in sentences:*
He *keeps an eye on* everything; for example; a less urgent job; watertight compartments; at heart; a fatherly interest; for this purpose; in case of doubt; he *looks* it *up* in the official guide; he *looks out for* the various papers (you have already had *look after, look through, look round*); he is saved the trouble.

III *Mark where the accent falls on each of the following words. Use each in a sentence:*

advertise, advertisement; telephone, telephonist; exports, exported; confirm, confirmation; continue, continuation; office, official.

IV *Answer the following:*

1. What are the responsibilities of the Office Manager? 2. Describe the duties of the mailing clerk. 3. How would you make

sure that the right enclosures go into the letters? 4. Is it necessary to write on a letter from England to Switzerland, 'By air mail'? 5. What is the cheapest way of sending a letter by air from England to South America? 6. Explain and discuss 'Flexibility is the essence of organisation'.

12
Commercial Correspondence

**layout   reference   incoming (outgoing) letters
complimentary close   Limited Company   per pro (p.p.)**

'What are you doing today?' asked Mr. Brown after Olaf had been in the office a few days.

'I am studying the incoming and outgoing letters,' answered Olaf. 'There is still a lot I have to learn about the general layout, which seems rather different from our style at home—the address, the reference, the paragraphs, the complimentary close, etc. I want to get absolutely perfect in everything connected with correspondence.'

'Excellent,' replied Mr. Brown. 'You have certainly got a good opportunity here to see all types of letters. Go ahead, and if you have any questions don't hesitate to ask me or any of the other people in the office.'

So Olaf set to work and made some careful notes. These are the things he noted:

General. Most of the letters were written in ordinary, good, straightforward English. One or two had some peculiar expressions and constructions, but these letters, Mr. Brown informed him, were from rather old-fashioned firms. He advised Olaf to avoid this form of 'Commercial English'; Weavewell's never used it.

'Our motto in letter writing,' said Mr. Brown, 'is: Remember the three C's—Clearness, Conciseness, Courtesy. I believe that in some American firms they have a motto like that hung up on the wall so that their employees are always reminded of it—a good idea.'

The Heading. Here is a characteristic heading:

Weavewell Woollen Co. Ltd.
Victoria Street,
London, EC4X ISH

Tel.: 01-173 7431 (6 lines)   **Telegrams: Weavewell, London**
Ref. GB/MC/E   **Telex: 7325149**

C. E. Eckersley, Esq.,   19th October, 19—.
c/o Longman Group Ltd.,
74, Grosvenor Street,
London, W1X 0AS

Dear Sir,

<u>AMERICAN SALES</u>

   In reply to your letter of 17th October (CEE/JW) we are pleased to inform you. . . .

Notes

1. *Limited* and *Company* are generally abbreviated *Ltd.* and *Co.* The majority of business firms are limited companies now; professional firms like solicitors and accountants, however, are mostly partnerships.

2. Notice that if an individual writes a formal letter, for example an application for a job, his name is not written above his address; and the address is typed in the top right-hand corner of the page. (See page 53.)

3. *Ref.* is the usual abbreviation for *Reference*. The letters mean that the letter was dictated by Mr. G. Brown, typed by Miss M. Carson and should be filed under the letter E. The reference is placed against the left-hand margin, either on the date line as above or at the foot of the letter (see p. 68). Where correspondence has already started, the reference of the letter to which

you are replying is often quoted in the opening paragraph as in the above example. Some firms make provision for it in their stationery, e.g.

Our Ref. . . . . .   Your Ref. . . . . . .   (Date)

(see letter on p. 110).

4. The name and address of the person to whom the letter is sent are generally put at the beginning of the letter on the left-hand side, as in the illustration. They are sometimes put at the end of the letter.

5. The abbreviation c/o means 'care of'. So if you wish to write to Mr. Eckersley at his publishers (the only address of his that you know) you address the letter to:

> C. E. Eckersley, Esq.,
> c/o Longman Group Ltd.,

Esq. is an abbreviation for *Esquire* (which nowadays doesn't mean anything very much). You could also write:

> Mr. C. E. Eckersley

You put either *Mr.* or *Esq.*, never both.

6. The date is written on the right of the letter and should be in one of these forms:

a) 19th October,[1] 1972;

b) October 19th, 1972.

The form 19/10/72 is sometimes used, but may give rise to misunderstandings: in the U.S.A. the same date would be written 10/19/72. Note, that when the ordinal numbers for the day of the month are used, the abbreviations for these are *1st, 2nd, 3rd, 4th, 5th,* etc.

7. *The Greeting.* The greeting should be made just under the inside address on the left-hand side. The usual greeting for one person is *Dear Sir* or *Dear Madam.*[2] If the person is well

---

[1] The following abbreviations for months are sometimes used; *Jan., Feb., Mar., Apr., Aug., Sept., Oct., Nov., Dec.* We do not abbreviate *May, June, July.*

[2] *Madam* is used in greeting for single as well as married women.

known to you and you have had frequent business dealings with him or her, you begin: *Dear Mr. Clifford*, or: *Dear Miss Jackson*.

The form *Sir* alone is not used in business letters, though it is the usual form in letters from government offices.

To a firm the usual greeting is *Dear Sirs* or occasionally *Gentlemen* (never *Dear Gentlemen*).

8. *Subject Line*. Sometimes it is useful to give some idea of the subject matter of the letter on a special subject line. This is generally placed between the greeting and the first paragraph of the letter as in the example on p. 46; it is usually typed in capitals and underlined.

9. *Opening Paragraph*. This is usually rather formal and will depend very much, of course, on the subject about which you are writing. It will probably begin by thanking the writer for his previous letter and mentioning the subject of it, e.g.

'Thank you for your letter of 15th May enquiring about our latest catalogue.'

10. Now follows the *Body* of the letter, which contains the actual information. It is essential and important to begin a new paragraph for each new subject; it makes the letter clearer and helps the person who receives it to answer point by point. On the other hand some writers have got into the habit of beginning a new paragraph with almost every sentence, which has exactly the opposite effect.

11. *Complimentary Close*. The usual ending for a business letter is *Yours faithfully* (this is the form most frequently used) or *Yours truly* or *Yours very truly*.[1] In more personal letters you use *Yours sincerely*. In general if the greeting is 'Dear Sir', the complimentary close will be 'Yours faithfully'; while 'Dear Mr. Clifford' would be followed by 'Yours sincerely'. Occasionally these endings are preceded by a phrase like *I am* or

---

[1] The Americans reverse this to *Very truly yours*, which is their favourite ending.

We remain because some writers feel that this makes the ending less abrupt. If the closing paragraph begins with a participle it *must* be followed by such a phrase, e.g.

>Awaiting your instructions,
>>We are,[1]
>>>Yours faithfully,

or: Thanking you for your assistance,

>>We remain,[1]
>>>Yours truly,

'... many signatures are not easy to read'

---

[1] These phrases are more frequently found in American business correspondence.

12. The *Signature* is always *written* even though the letter is typed, but as many signatures are not always easy to read, the name is often typed under the signature, e.g.

    Yours faithfully,

    W. Kaufmann (signature)

    W. Kaufmann

Generally a director or a principal of the firm signs all important letters, writing his name beneath the typed name of the firm, e.g.

    Yours faithfully,
    WEAVEWELL WOOLLEN CO. LTD.
    S. RUSHTON
    Director

If a manager or the head of a department signs for the firm he will do it like this:

    For WEAVEWELL WOOLLEN CO. LTD.,
    B. HAMMOND
    Export Manager

or   per pro[1] WEAVEWELL WOOLLEN CO. LTD.,
    G. BROWN
    Office Manager

---

[1] *per pro.* or often just *p.p.* stands for the Latin *per procurationem* and means that the person is authorised to sign for the firm. *For and on behalf of* has the same meaning; both forms are frequently used on cheques, bills of exchange and other documents.

COMMERCIAL CORRESPONDENCE

13. *The Envelope*. The address should begin about halfway down the envelope and should be arranged something like this:

C. Ewart, Esq.,
  The Pines,
    Oxshott Road,
      Canterbury,
        Kent.
	Messrs. Jackett & Lane Ltd.,[1]
	29, Park Ridge Road,
	London, EC5Y 2SO

Sir Charles Northwood,
  Thackeray House,
    Queensway,
London, W2A 3ML
	The Reina Linen Co. Ltd.,[2]
	Purley Way,
	Knightstown,
	Lancs.

N.B.

1. *Messrs.* stands for *Messieurs* (which is never written in full in English. Neither is *Mister* or *Mistress*; they are always, in addresses or greetings, abbreviated to *Mr.* ['mistə] and *Mrs.* ['misiz]).

2. The following abbreviations are sometimes used: *Rd.* for *Road*; *St.* for *Street*; *Av.* for *Avenue*; *Sq.* for *Square*; *Pl.* for *Place*; *Gdns.* for *Gardens*; *Pk.* for *Park*; *Terr.* for *Terrace*; *Cres.* for *Crescent*; *Ho.* for *House*.

Exercises

I WORD STUDY. *Use each of the following:*

close (noun, verb, and (with a different pronunciation) adjective; [klouz] noun and verb, [klous] adjective), paragraph, hesitate (also *hesitant, hesitation*), straightforward, peculiar, construction (also *construct, constructive*; give the opposite of each), old-fashioned (an opposite is *up-to-date*), motto, concise, courtesy (what is the corresponding adjective?), characteristic, heading, abbreviate (give the corresponding noun), nowadays, custom (and *customary*; use also *customer*), ordinal numbers (give the first four *ordinal* and the first four *cardinal* numbers), greeting,

---

[1] Note the two forms of layout for an address.
[2] Note that *Messrs.* is not used for impersonal firm-names.

regret, principal (as a noun and as an adjective; compare with *principle*), 'stand for'; layout (is this the same as *outlay*?).

II *Answer the following:*
1. In what sort of English ought a business letter to be written?
2. What were Mr. Brown's 'three Cs' for business letters?
3. What do the following abbreviations stand for: Ltd., Co., Ref., No., c/o, Esq., per pro, Messrs.?
4. What is the difference between *Yours faithfully* and *Yours sincerely*?
5. Where in the letter do you put the name and address of the person to whom it is sent?

III *Set out the following headings, greetings and complimentary closes correctly, putting in the necessary punctuation. Use the firm's notepaper; consult the examples on pages 46-51 of this book:*

a. horrocks and coates ltd cloth manufacturers 34 hagden lane bradford bd2 4bb ref sm/L. 27th april 19— dear sirs. . . . yours faithfully b jones sales manager.
b. morgan and parker ltd 18 king street leicester ref PD/E 9th march 19— midland counties transport co ltd queen street bristol dear sirs. . . . yours faithfully p.p. morgan and parker p davis manager.
c. the reliance trading co ltd park street birmingham ref CE/1 29th oct 19— j hardman esq cathedral st exeter dear sir . . . we remain yours truly for reliance trading company r wigfield director encl.

IV *Write the following letters:*
1. To a firm of stationers ordering 500 sheets of writing paper (give size and quality) and 500 envelopes.
2. A reply from a firm of stationers.

13
Applications for a Job

book-keeping   testimonial   diploma   shorthand

Among the letters which especially interested Olaf were those applications he had seen on the first day. They had been written in reply to this advertisement that had appeared in *The Times* two or three days before he had started work:

WANTED by City firm of Textile Wholesalers efficient shorthand-typist (lady)[1]. Knowledge of book-keeping an advantage. Applications stating age and experience to Box 6942.

Here are some of the applications which Olaf read carefully before they were filed under 'Staff Applications':

14, Park Avenue,[2]
Wembley,
Middlesex.
17th October, 19—.

Box No. 6942,
The Times Publishing Company Ltd.,
Printing House Square,
London, EC4P 4DE

Dear Sir,
  In reply to your advertisement in *The Times* I should be

[1] Not all firms nowadays demand that typists should be able to take shorthand, and they may advertise for 'audio-typists', trained to type from dictating machines. Mr. Brown believes in moving with the times, and dictaphones are widely used at Weavewell's; but he still prefers his secretaries to be able to take shorthand when the need arises (for example when he wishes notes to be taken at a meeting, or if there is a power cut).

[2] In a letter from a private individual, the writer's name is not put above his or her address (see page 46).

grateful if you would consider my application for this post.[1]

I have been working as a shorthand-typist for more than seven years; my speed in shorthand is 120 words per minute[2] and in typing 50 words per minute. I am experienced in all kinds of office work and have a good knowledge of accountancy. My age is 25.

I enclose copies of three testimonials and hope that you will give me the opportunity of an interview.

Yours faithfully,
JEAN SIMMONS

Encl. 3 copies.

14, Wilson Place,
London, N4M 2CP
16th October, 19—.

Box 6942,
The Times,
London, EC4P 4DE
Dear Sir,

With reference to your advertisement for a shorthand-typist I wish to apply for this job.

After leaving school, where I passed the G.C.E. ('O' level)[3] in four subjects (English Language, English Literature, French and Mathematics), I entered a firm of importers of glass and

---

[1] *Post*, here = position; job.

[2] Notice that speeds are measured in words per minute, not letters per minute.

[3] G.C.E. ('O' level) = General Certificate of Education, 'Ordinary' level— an examination taken at about the age of 16 in England and Wales. It is not necessary to pass a certain number of subjects: the individual subjects passed are credited to the candidate, and failures in other subjects do not count against him. The other English school examinations are the G.C.E. 'A' (= 'Advanced') level, and the C.S.E. (Certificate of Secondary Education).

china for whom I have worked for nine years. Unfortunately, they have to reduce their staff because of import restrictions and I have, therefore, to look for new employment.

I am well qualified in shorthand (140) and typewriting (60). For the last three years I have worked part-time in the Accounts Department and have a fair knowledge of book-keeping.

I shall be 26 years of age on 24th November of this year.

                         Yours faithfully,
                         MARY GAMMONS

                         6, Bramsford Gdns.,
                         London, NW3A 2KW.
                         16th October, 19—.

Box 6942,
The Times,
London, EC4P 4DE.
Dear Sirs,

I have seen your advertisement in *The Times* of today, and wish to apply for the post of shorthand-typist.

I enclose a full *curriculum vitae*, together with copies of my Diploma and testimonial from the Hayward School of Commerce. The Principal, Miss Parker, will be pleased to give you any further information you may wish to have about my character or my work.

I am most anxious to supplement my theoretical knowledge with practical experience, and should be very grateful for a favourable consideration of my application.

                         Yours faithfully,
Encl.   *HELEN PRIOR*

CURRICULUM VITAE

Name:	Helen Prior
Address:	6, Bramsford Gardens, London, NW3A 2KW
Date of birth:	14th June, 19—
Status:	Single
Education:	Northway Comprehensive School Hayward School of Commerce

Qualifications:	C.S.E.[1] in English, Mathematics (Grade 1) and Geography (Grade 2)
	Hayward School of Commerce Diploma:
	    Shorthand—Good
	    Typing—Good
	    Book-keeping—Very Good
	    English—Very Good

Experience:	None
Interests:	Travel, music, swimming (North London Swimming Club)
Referee:	Miss Mary Parker, B.A., Principal, The Hayward School of Commerce, Wimbledon, SW18L 4UN

---

[1] See page 54.

Testimonial

**The Hayward School of Commerce,
Wimbledon,
SW18L 4UN.**

20th September, 19—

TO WHOM IT MAY CONCERN

Miss HELEN PRIOR, aged 17, attended a commercial course at this college from 15th September 19— to 14th September 19—. She was awarded the school's Diploma, in which she gained particularly good results in book-keeping and English.

Miss Prior was always a courteous and willing student who took a keen interest in college activities, and I have every confidence that she will make a reliable and pleasant secretary.

MARY PARKER,
Principal.

Olaf looked with interest at the diploma, testimonial and *curriculum vitae* enclosed in the third letter.

'Well, Petersen,' said Mr. Brown. 'What do you think of them? Which would you choose?'

'Honestly, I don't know, Mr. Brown. I think I should ask all three to come for an interview—or to send a photograph!'

Mr. Brown laughed. 'That's just what I am going to do—ask them to come for an interview, I mean. But when I choose one, it probably won't be for the reason that you would. I want efficiency as well as good looks. Now you can write a letter to each (the same letter will do for all three, with the name changed, of course), asking them to come for an interview next Thursday at 3.30. Show me the letter before it goes out.'

After some effort, and a few corrections by Mr. Brown, this is what Olaf sent:

Weavewell Woollen Co. Ltd.
Victoria Street,
London, EC4X 1SH

GB/MC 21st October, 19—.

Miss Jean Simmons,
14, Park Avenue,
Wembley, Middlesex.

Dear Madam,

Thank you for your letter applying for the post of typist. I should be glad if you could come here for an interview on Thursday next, 29th October, at 3.30. If that day or time is not convenient, will you kindly let me know, and I will try to arrange the interview for some other day and time suitable to both of us.

Yours faithfully,
p.p. Weavewell Woollen Co. Ltd.
G. BROWN
Office Manager

Exercises

I WORD STUDY. *Use the following:*

efficient (also *efficiency* and *inefficient*), grateful (give the negative. What is the corresponding noun? Give its negative), speed, pass (here 'be successful in'; notice the difference between 'to take an examination' and 'to pass an examination'), china (mention three articles of china), reduce (give the corresponding noun), restrict (also *restrictions*), part-time (what is the opposite?), choose (give the parts of the verb and the corresponding noun), photograph, effort, convenient (give the opposite).

II *Put in the missing prepositions or adverbs:*

1. The letters were written —— reply —— an advertisement —— *The Times*.

APPLICATIONS FOR A JOB

2. —— reference —— your advertisement —— a shorthand-typist I wish to apply —— this job.
3. —— leaving school —— the age —— 16, I entered a firm —— importers —— glass —— whom I have worked —— nine years.
4. I should be grateful —— a favourable consideration —— my application.
5. Thank you —— your letter —— 19th October applying —— the above situation.
6. I should be glad if you could come here —— an interview —— Thursday, 29th October, —— 3.30.

III *Answer the following:*

1. If you wanted to find a job what would you do?
2. How do you address your letter when a Box No. is given?
3. If you were writing a letter applying for a post, what points would you think it important your letter should contain?
4. What system of shorthand is generally used in your country?[1]
5. What is an 'audio-typist'?
6. What is a power cut?

IV *Your firm wants a filing clerk. Write:*

a. a suitable advertisement for your newspaper;
b. a letter of application for the post;
c. a letter from the firm asking the applicant to come for an interview;
d. a letter from the firm telling the applicant that he (or she) has *not* been given the position.

[1] In England the usual one is Pitman's.

14
The Sales Department

---

statistics   pattern book   delivery date   pigeon-holes   stock label

For more than six weeks now Olaf has worked under Mr. Brown's supervision and has learned a lot during that time. One day Miss Carson fell ill and he had to take over the filing; he was surprised how well he managed. His good memory helped him to remember firms and addresses, and he was by now quite familiar with most of the names of the regular customers and suppliers.

That was most useful when Mr. Brown asked him to take Miss Clarke's place at the switchboard during lunch-time. Fortunately, there were not so many calls between 1 o'clock and 2 o'clock, and after the first few days Olaf got on well. There was one little difficulty he ran up against. As so many heads of

'. . . one little difficulty he ran up against'

departments and members of the staff were out during that hour, he could not put the calls through to them, so he had to take messages. Weavewell's had special forms for telephone messages;

APPLICATIONS FOR A JOB

but Olaf found it quite a job to listen, to answer and to fill in the form at the same time. (He had to note the date, the time of the call, the caller's name and the message, and then hand the form to the persons concerned when they came in.)

On days when Mr. Brown was very busy or had a meeting with the manager or the directors he asked Olaf to attend to the mail. Then, one morning early in December, Mr. Brown said to him: 'Look, Petersen, I think you have now got the hang of[1] this department and if you like I'll have a word with Mr. Clifford and suggest that you put in some time now in the Sales Department.'

And so, next morning, Olaf reported to Mr. Austin, the Sales Manager, whom he had, of course, seen almost daily and with whom he got on very well. 'Well, Petersen,' he said, 'your father and I are old friends; we've done business together for the last twenty years, and I'll certainly do all I can to show you how we run this department. You are the son of a business man, so I needn't tell you how important the Sales Department is. Of course, other departments are necessary too, but they would soon have to close down if we didn't do our job properly here. Well, I believe in practical work. I don't want to confuse you by explaining too many things at once. So we'd better begin with the home trade. Mr. Hammond will show you the organisation (and the complications) of the export trade later.'

OLAF: Have you got separate departments for home and export?

MR. AUSTIN: Well, they are not really separate departments; they are both under my control, but the conditions are so different in many respects that we found it an advantage to have one man specialising in exports only, whilst I concentrate mainly on the home market. But, of course, Mr. Hammond and I work in close co-operation.

OLAF: And what do you call the home market?

MR. AUSTIN: Well, all sales in the British Isles (and that includes

[1] *to get the hang of* = to understand.

the whole of Ireland) we call home sales. And for our statistics—we shall come to that later—we sub-divide them into town and country sales. Town is the entire London area, and everything outside that is country.

Now let us see what is in today's mail. Perhaps we'd better go through the inquiries first because, after all, most sales begin with an inquiry. There are always a number of inquiries in the post every day. Some come from old, well-known customers, others come from firms we know, but have not done business with yet, and sometimes we get an inquiry from a firm we have never heard of. There are customers who state clearly and exactly what they want (the efficient ones, as a rule), and others who are so vague that we have more or less to guess what to offer them. That's where the personal knowledge of the customer and of the type of his business is so useful. You must always remember that every inquiry is a potential sale and it is our job to make it a sale by treating it individually. So in most cases I send a personal letter with the samples, because I believe that this little personal touch makes all the difference.

OLAF: But how do you select the samples, Mr. Austin. You cannot possibly know all the hundreds of articles and qualities by heart?

MR. AUSTIN: Well, it's surprising how much one can remember. But look at these pattern books.

With these words he took Olaf to a big table on which some enormous books were lying. He explained that in these books was a pattern of every kind of cloth the firm had in stock or on order, with the number, the price, the delivery date or any other necessary information. From these books he marks every inquiry with the distinguishing numbers of the articles which he thinks will meet the customer's requirements.

These inquiries are then passed to the pattern room, and Mr. Austin showed Olaf the shelves with hundreds of pigeon-holes where the patterns are kept in numerical order. They are all

THE SALES DEPARTMENT

labelled and numbered and can be looked out very quickly. The pattern clerk is in charge and a typist writes the price lists for him.

Exercises

I WORD STUDY. *Use the following:*

supervision (also *supervise, supervisor*), memory (and *remember*), job (note the two uses in this chapter):
1. Olaf *found it quite a job* to listen, to answer and to fill in the form at the same time.
2. They would soon have to close down if we didn't *do our job* properly here.

specialise (also *special* ['speʃl], *specialist, speciality* [speʃi'æliti], *specialisation* [speʃəlai'zeiʃn]), concentrate (and *concentration*), co-operation, isles (and *island* ['ailənd]), vague, potential, individually, enormous, requirements (also *require*), pigeon-holes.

II IDIOMS AND PHRASES. *Note the following and use in sentences of your own:*

under Mr. Brown's *supervision*; Miss Carson *fell ill*; Olaf *had to take over* the filing; he *took Miss Clarke's place*; Olaf *got on well*; to *fill in the form*; you have now *got the hang of* this department; you can *put in some time* now with Mr. Austin; if we didn't do our job other departments would *have to close down*; we had (*we'd*) *better* begin with the home trade; we have *more or less* to guess what to offer them; in these books is a pattern of every kind of cloth the firm has *in stock* or *on order*; they can be *looked out* very quickly; the pattern clerk is *in charge*.

III *Answer the following:*

1. What details would you fill in on a telephone message form? 2. What are the two branches of trade? 3. What, in England, is meant by 'home trade'? 4. What is the difference between 'town' and 'country' sales? 5. What is a pattern book?

IV *Write a short essay on the following:*

The work of the Sales Department.

15
Correspondence of the Sales Department (1)

quotation   turnover   receipt   discount   competitive

'Now, Petersen,' said Mr. Austin, 'here are yesterday's inquiries from old customers, and attached to them the answers I have dictated. Have a good look at them. They are all a little bit different from each other.'

Inquiry

R. L. Street & Co. Ltd.

**156, North Street,
Chester, CH2 1GS**

8th December, 19—.

Weavewell Woollen Co. Ltd.,
Victoria Street,
London, EC4X 1SH

Dear Sirs,
   We are interested in navy and black worsteds and should be pleased if you would send us patterns of good and medium qualities which you can supply from stock.
   If you give us a really competitive quotation we may place a substantial order.

>   Yours faithfully,
>   For R. L. Street & Co. Ltd.
>   *P. HARRIS*

Reply

Weavewell Woollen Co. Ltd.
Victoria Street,
London, EC4X 1SH

9th December, 19—.

DA/LR
Messrs. R. L. Street & Co. Ltd.,
156, North Street,
Chester, CH2 1GS

Dear Sirs,

We are obliged for your letter of 8th December and are sending you under separate cover our price list and patterns of navy and black worsteds.

All these materials are made of the finest pure wool. Some of them you have had from us before, and know, therefore, how readily they sell.

We are keen to expand our turnover with you, and have given you what we feel is an extremely competitive quotation. Our orders are very heavy, however, and we cannot guarantee that we shall be able to repeat these prices when present stocks are exhausted.

We look forward to giving your order our most careful attention.

Yours faithfully,
p.p. Weavewell Woollen Co. Ltd.
D. AUSTIN
Sales Manager

CHAPTER 15

'Our orders are very heavy . . .'

Inquiry

S. G. Hamilton & Co.
64, Newgate,
Southport, PR8 1DH

8th December, 19—.

Weavewell Woollen Co. Ltd.,
Victoria Street,
London, EC4X 1SH

Dear Sirs,
    Kindly send us as soon as possible patterns of grey flannels with your lowest prices. Prompt delivery is essential.

                      Yours faithfully,
               For S. G. Hamilton & Co.
                   S. LLOYD

Reply

Weavewell Woollen Co. Ltd.
Victoria Street,
London, EC4X 1SH

DA/LR 9th December, 19—.

Messrs. S. G. Hamilton & Co.,
64, Newgate,
Southport, PR8 1DH

Dear Sirs,

We thank you for your inquiry of 8th December for grey flannels, and have pleasure in sending you patterns of various qualities of cloth which we can supply from stock.

Though prices have gone up steadily since September we have managed to hold our quotations down, and we hope that you will let us have your order before further rises in costs make increases unavoidable.

    Yours faithfully,
   p.p. Weavewell Woollen Co. Ltd.
    D. AUSTIN
    Sales Manager

Encl.

Weavewell Woollen Co. Ltd.
Victoria Street,
London, EC4X 1SH

PRICE LIST

9th December, 19—.

Messrs. S. G. Hamilton & Co.,
64, Newgate,
Southport, PR8 1DH

Quality	Width	Weight	Price	Delivery
8008	56	14/15	£1.63	prompt
8054	56	15/16	£1.70	,,
8059	56	15/16	£1.81	,,
9010	58/60	16/18	£2.14	,,

30 days 2%, 60 days net.

Inquiry

Brown & Carter Ltd.

Ushfield House,
Liverpool, L3 3TC

8th December, 19—.

Weavewell Woollen Co. Ltd.,
Victoria Street,
London, EC4X 1SH

Dear Sirs,

Exp. 4022

We have an export inquiry for grey gaberdine qualities and would ask you to let us have by return patterns of materials of which you have at least 4 or 5 pieces[1] in stock.

We trust that you will make an effort to quote us your most favourable terms for big quantities.

Yours faithfully,
For Brown & Carter Ltd.

H. GRIGSON

HG/RS

---

[1] A piece is 45 to 50 yards. International trade is now fully metricated, but for the home trade Weavewell's still quote in the old English measures of yards, feet and inches, and pounds and ounces (see p. 151).

Reply

Weavewell Woollen Co. Ltd.
Victoria Street,
London, EC4X 1SH

DA/LR   9th December, 19—.

Messrs. Brown & Carter Ltd.,
Ushfield House,
Liverpool, L3 3TC

Dear Sirs,

Exp. 4022

We acknowledge with thanks the receipt of your letter of 8th December and have pleasure in enclosing our patterns of grey gaberdine. We are sure that you will find something to suit your customer here; quality No. 7624 has had particularly good overseas sales recently.

On the attached price list we have given our very lowest quotations; for orders of 2 pieces and more we shall allow you a special discount of $2\frac{1}{2}\%$.

All qualities can at present be supplied from stock, but in view of the keen demand we would advise you to send us your order without delay.

                                 Yours faithfully,
                       p.p. Weavewell Woollen Co. Ltd.
                                 D. AUSTIN
                                 Sales Manager

Encl.

Exercises

I WORD STUDY. *Use each of the following:*

medium, substantial, competitive (use also *compete* [kəm'pi:t], *competition* [kɔmpə'tiʃn]), navy (here it means *navy blue*, i.e. a very dark blue), readily (use also *ready*), exhausted (here it means *sold out*. Use it in its general meaning), prompt, delivery (use also *deliver*), recommend (also *recommendation*), width (give the corresponding adjective. What are the corresponding adjectives to *length, height, depth, breadth*?), advantage (also *advantageous*. Use also *to take advantage of*), receipt [ri'si:t] (what is the corresponding verb? What is *a recipe* ['resipi]? What is *a prescription*?).

II *In this chapter there were a number of characteristic phrases used in Commercial Correspondence. Try to remember them. Use these in sentences of your own:*

1. We should be obliged if you would; 2. which you can supply from stock; 3. a really competitive quotation; 4. we may place a substantial order; 5. under separate cover; 6. to expand our turnover; 7. our present stocks are exhausted; 8. we look forward to receiving your order; 9. shall give your order our most careful attention; 10. with your lowest prices; 11. prompt delivery; 12. pleasure in sending you; 13. patterns of various qualities; 14. prices have gone up; 15. let us have your order; 16. by return; 17. quote us; 18. your most favourable terms; 19. acknowledge the receipt of your letter; 20. the attached price-list; 21. a special discount of $2\frac{1}{2}\%$.

III *The following are notes of letters. Write them out fully:*

1a. To: The Star Pottery Co., Stoke-on-Trent.

Have received export inquiry for 500 cups and saucers—white, gold pattern—samples by return—quotation—immediate delivery required.

Goswell China Co., Liverpool.

b. To: Goswell China Co., Liverpool.

Thanks for inquiry—samples 6 different patterns and qualities sent with price list—500 of any supplied from stock—hope receive order—will have immediate attention.

2a. To: Brazilian Steamship Co., Rio de Janeiro.

Cargo of goods next month—15th May shipment to England—weight 5 tons—date of sailings Rio–London—quotation for cost.

b. To: Copacabana Rubber Co.

Steamship *Amazon* leaving Rio 15th May—arrive London 31st May—Goods collected and loaded by Brazilian Steamship Co. 14th May—cost £3 per ton.

IV 1a. Write a letter of inquiry to Weavewell's asking for quotations and patterns of cloth suitable for men's suits in your country.

b. Write a reply from the Sales Manager of Weavewell's.

2a. Write to the Argentine Shipping Company, St. Paul's Street, London, for details of their sailings to Buenos Aires.

b. Write the reply from the Company.

3a. Write an enquiry to British Leyland Motor Corporation, Oxford, from The Iranian Garage Co., Teheran, Iran, asking for their latest price list, discount, and date of delivery of cars.

b. Write the reply from the Sales Department of B.L.M.C.

4a. The firm of which you are Secretary wants to give a dinner to celebrate its 50th year of business. Write an inquiry to a big hotel asking for a quotation for 100 guests.

b. Write the reply of the Manager of the hotel.

5. Your firm wants a new system of electric lighting put into its offices. Write to the Neon Electric Company explaining what you want and asking for a quotation.

16
Correspondence of the Sales Department (2)

**representative   range   calculation   margin   references
status inquiry   credit limit**

The inquiries that appear on pages 64 to 68 are, of course, the easiest type of inquiry: the customer is known, his requirements are clearly stated and the firm can offer what is wanted.

In other cases, however, it is a little more complicated: customers ask for articles which are out of stock or for terms which cannot be granted. In such cases great tact and care are needed not to lose the order or to upset the customer.

'... not to lose the order or to upset the customer'

CORRESPONDENCE OF THE SALES DEPARTMENT (2)

Here are two inquiries with the respective replies:

Inquiry

John Jackman & Co.
Dovey Street,
Leominster, HR7 2PR

9th December, 19—.

Weavewell Woollen Co. Ltd.,
Victoria Street,
London, EC4X 1SH

Dear Sirs,

When your representative called here some time ago he showed us a Velour 'Specia'. We could not give him an order then, but told him that we might be interested later. We have now enlarged our dress-goods department and are considering the addition of new qualities to our stocks. Your Velour 'Specia' would fit in well. Please send us a large cutting and patterns of the complete range of colours which are in production. We expect you to quote your very lowest prices and would like to know whether you can supply from stock.

If we decide to introduce your quality we want your assurance that you will not sell it to other firms in Leominster.

We look forward to your early reply,

and remain,

Yours faithfully,
For John Jackman & Co.
P. KENDALL

PK/BD

Reply

Weavewell Woollen Co. Ltd.
Victoria Street,
London, EC4X 1SH

DA/LR 10th December, 19—.

Messrs. John Jackman & Co.,
Dovey Street,
Leominster, HR7 2PR

Dear Sirs,

We thank you for your letter of 9th December in which you inquire about our Velour 'Specia'.

We appreciate your interest; and, while we can no longer supply 'Specia' from stock as the range has been discontinued, we are sure that you will find our new material, 'Spectre', an excellent replacement. The finish has been greatly improved at very little extra cost, and sales so far suggest that this will be another 'best-seller'.

We are sending you under separate cover, 'samples without value', half a yard full width with our full range of colours. Our best prices are noted on the enclosed list, and goods can be delivered within two weeks of receipt of your order.

Your request to be given the exclusive sale for Leominster is somewhat unusual. As we are very keen to increase our turnover with you we are, however, willing to grant this concession provided you place an initial order for no fewer than 30 pieces.

We are certain that you will find a ready sale for this excellent quality and feel sure that it will give you every satisfaction.

We have informed our representative, Mr. Charles Amery, of your inquiry, and he will call on you in the near future. We are looking forward to hearing from you.

> Yours faithfully,
> p.p. Weavewell Woollen Co. Ltd.
> *D. AUSTIN*
> Sales Manager

Encl.

Inquiry

Murphy & Hale Ltd.
**16, Barnstaple Road,
Exeter, EX3 6NH**

9th December, 19—.

Weavewell Woollen Co. Ltd.,
Victoria Street,
London, EC4X 1SH

Dear Sirs,

We are pleased to inform you that the quality 'Elasto' which we bought from you in September has sold very well.

We are considering making it one of our standard qualities if you can give us a trade discount of 5%. We feel that our regular orders would be well worth such a concession and are awaiting your reply with interest.

> Yours faithfully,
> Murphy & Hale Ltd.
> *ALLAN HALE*
> Director

AH/WP

Reply

Weavewell Woollen Co. Ltd.
Victoria Street,
London, EC4X ISH

DA/LR
                                      10th December, 19—.

Messrs. Murphy & Hale Ltd.,
16, Barnstaple Road,
Exeter, EX3 6NH

Dear Sirs,

We acknowledge with thanks your letter of 9th December and are glad to hear from you that our quality 'Elasto' is selling so well.

We appreciate your suggestion that you should make 'Elasto' one of your standard qualities, but regret very much that it is impossible for us to grant you a reduction of 5%. A cash discount of $2\frac{1}{2}$% can, of course, be deducted from all payments made within 30 days.

'Elasto' at its present price is, in our opinion, superior to any similar fabric on the market, and we are convinced that it would benefit your sales if you stocked it regularly.

Owing to the very heavy demand and the orders we are booking every day, we can accept orders only for delivery March/April and would therefore ask you to let us know your requirements as soon as possible.

                       Yours faithfully,
                 p.p. Weavewell Woollen Co. Ltd.
                    D. AUSTIN
                    Sales Manager

CORRESPONDENCE OF THE SALES DEPARTMENT (2)

There is another class of inquiries which is perhaps the most important one: inquiries from new customers. It is, of course, the constant aim of the Sales Manager to increase his circle of customers, and such an inquiry, therefore, will always receive special attention. Mr. Austin shows Olaf this letter:

Inquiry

Reynold & Harvey
14, King Street,
Coventry, CV5 4MB

JR/HG 9th December, 19—.
Weavewell Woollen Co. Ltd.,
Victoria Street,
London, EC4X 1SH

Dear Sirs,
  We have seen your advertisement in the 'Textile World' and should be glad if you would send us patterns of Ladies' Woollens with your best terms.

  Yours faithfully,
  Reynold & Harvey
  J. REYNOLD

Mr. Austin explains to Olaf that he knows the firm well, and that he and the traveller have tried several times to open an account with them; but without success. Now, quite unexpectedly, they are writing in reply to an advertisement. The inquiry is very general, but Mr. Austin very carefully selects some of the best articles from the firm's range and writes the following letter with the offer:

Reply

Weavewell Woollen Co. Ltd.
Victoria Street,
London, EC4X 1SH

DA/LR
10th December, 19—.

Messrs. Reynold & Harvey,
14, King Street,
Coventry, CV5 4MB

Dear Sirs,

Thank you for your inquiry of 9th December for Ladies' Woollens.

We have much pleasure in sending you a full selection of our latest and best-selling designs and hope that some of them will interest you.

May we draw your special attention to our exclusive quality 'Goldring' which has been an outstanding success. We believe that it represents the best value for money in this type of goods and we are sure that you will find that it sells very well indeed.

If the range of patterns which we have selected does not contain everything you want, please do not hesitate to let us know your exact requirements: we are most anxious to meet your wishes.

We are looking forward to receiving your order, which shall have our best attention.

Yours faithfully,
p.p. Weavewell Woollen Co. Ltd.
D. AUSTIN
Sales Manager

Encl.

Another inquiry that had come a few days ago was from a firm which was unknown to Mr. Austin. In that case it was necessary to ask for references to find out whether the financial standing of the firm justified credit terms. We shall see later how status inquiries are dealt with and how the credit limit is fixed by the Sales Manager.[1] Here is the inquiry:

Inquiry

John Sterling & Co.
Market Place,
Norwich, NOR1 5JC

Our Ref.   Your Ref.
HS/FK   ....   3rd December, 19—.
Weavewell Woollen Co. Ltd.,
Victoria Street,
London, EC4X 1SH

Dear Sirs,
    At last year's British Textiles Fair we saw your stand on which you were showing your 'Goldring' fabrics. Would you please send us patterns of this quality and quote your best prices.
Yours faithfully,
pp. John Sterling & Co.
H. STREET

---

[1] See page 175ff.

Reply

Weavewell Woollen Co. Ltd.
Victoria Street,
London, EC4X ISH

DA/LR 5th December, 19—.
Messrs. John Sterling & Co.,
Market Place,
Norwich, NOR1 5JC

Dear Sirs,

We are much obliged for your letter of 3rd December inquiring about our quality 'Goldring'.

Under separate cover we are sending you our spring range for delivery January to March. We have quoted our best terms on the enclosed price list and trust that you will agree that the price for this excellent quality is extremely low. As a matter of fact, we may soon have to raise it because the price of raw materials has been rising steadily for the last two months.

Our traveller for Norfolk will be in Norwich in the second half of January. We have informed him of your inquiry[1] and he will write to you some time before his visit in order to fix an appointment.

As we have not yet an account with you, we should be glad if you would kindly let us have the usual references.

We want to assure you that any order that you may place with us shall receive our careful attention.

Yours faithfully,
p.p. Weavewell Woollen Co. Ltd.
D. AUSTIN

Encl. Sales Manager

---

[1] A copy of the letter is sent to the traveller.

Exercises

I WORD STUDY. *Use the following:*

tact (also *tactful*), manufacture (also *manufacturer* and *factory*), similar, slightly, expensive (what is the opposite?), approve (also *approval*), district, concession [kən'seʃn] (the corresponding verb is *concede* [kən'siːd]), grant, reduction (what is the corresponding verb? What is the opposite of *reduction*?), absorb, deduct (also *deduction*), superior (what is the opposite?), fabric, constant, design (noun and verb), exclusive (what is the opposite?), outstanding, financial (use also *finance*, noun and verb), fair (noun; *fair* is also an adjective with three different meanings, all commonly used. Can you give them?), advantageous, raw materials (what is *raw* meat?), furnish (what does *to furnish a house* mean?).

II *Note and learn the following phrases from letters in Chapter 16. Use them in sentences of your own:*

1. We appreciate your interest; 2. from stock; 3. at little extra cost; 4. selling extremely well; 5. we are sure; 6. orders can be delivered; 7. on receipt of your order; 8. within two weeks of order; 9. place an initial order; 10. give you every satisfaction; 11. inform our representative; 12. in the near future; 13. we are looking forward to; 14. we are considering making; 15. give us a trade discount; 16. well worth such a concession; 17. we much appreciate; 18. to grant a reduction; 19. regret very much; 20. it is impossible for us to grant you a reduction; 21. superior to any on the market; 22. owing to the heavy demand; 23. as soon as possible; 24. we hope that some of them will interest you; 25. draw your special attention to; 26. an outstanding success; 27. represents the best value for money; 28. the range of patterns; 29. please do not hesitate; 30. kindly let us have the usual references; 31. under separate cover.

III *Expand the following notes of letters:*

1a. To: The Colibri Lighter Co. Ltd.,
    Walmer House,
    288-292, Regent Street,
    London, W.1.   *19th August*, 19—.

Bought 50 of your 'Colibri Original' models last May—best lighter we have ever had—sold very well—consider making special show of this model—willing to take 300 if special trade discount of 5%—are 'Colibri' prepared to grant this?—await reply.

MURRAY & BROWN LTD.,
Leicester.

b. To: Murray & Brown Ltd.,
    Leicester.

Thanks for letter 18th January—pleased to hear success of 'Colibri Original'—appreciate suggestion of special show—will send publicity material—greatly regret discount 5% impossible—margin of profit kept very small to keep down price—allow $2\frac{1}{2}\%$ cash discount 30 days—selling well everywhere—very heavy demand—if want 300 necessary give order by return—delivery date Oct./Nov. Awaiting reply.

2a. To: Queenly Stocking Co. Ltd.,
     Cobham, Surrey.

Seen advert in 'Hosier's Journal'—send price list—place order for 500 pairs if terms satisfactory—quote discount allowed and most advantageous terms.

E. CHARLES & CO.,
Knightstown.

b. To: E. Charles & Co. Ltd.,
    Knightstown.

Much obliged for letter—sending price list under separate cover—believe prices exceedingly low for quality of goods—costs rising—labour and raw materials—may have to increase prices—informed traveller of inquiry—will call next month—write fixing appointment. Not yet account—please give us usual references. Any order careful attention.

QUEENLY STOCKING CO. LTD.

IV *Write the following:*

1a. From a customer to your firm giving an order for an article that you no longer manufacture.
 b. A reply suggesting another similar but better article.
2a. From a good customer to your firm asking for a special discount for a large order.
 b. Your reply stating as tactfully as you can that you are unable to grant the discount.

3a. An inquiry from your firm asking for a price list and samples of goods advertised in your trade paper by a firm with whom you have not previously done business.
 b. Your reply, suggest references.
4a. To the Eastern Electric Co., Grays, Essex, asking for further details about a television set advertised in the morning paper.
 b. A reply from the Secretary of the Eastern Electric Company giving particulars and inviting you to come and see the set working. Use the firm's notepaper.
5. To a retail business firm sending them your firm's latest catalogue and pointing out some new types of goods.

17
Some Explanations. Sales Promotion

---

net   cash discount   trade discount   profit   firm offer
on approval   sales promotion   'prospect'   'follow-up'
agent   expenses   commission   conference   show card
bulk orders

OLAF: Have you got a few minutes to spare, Mr. Austin? I should like to ask you some questions on points I did not quite understand in the letters you gave me to read.

MR. AUSTIN: Certainly, I'll be only too pleased if I can help you. What is it?

OLAF: You see, I got a little confused with the expressions 'terms' and 'discount'; they seem to have several meanings.

MR. AUSTIN: So they have. Strictly speaking, terms are the conditions of payment. If you see a price list marked: Terms 30 days 5%, 60 days $2\frac{1}{2}$%, 90 days net, that means that the customer can deduct 5% cash discount if he pays within 30 days, but only $2\frac{1}{2}$% within 60 days, and if he pays after two months he loses the cash discount altogether. After 90 days payment is overdue. Very often, however, the word 'terms' is used in a wider sense and includes the price of the goods. So when the customers ask for your best terms, they mean the lowest price and the highest cash discount.

OLAF: But in some cases they ask for a trade discount; what does that mean?

MR. AUSTIN: Oh, that is entirely different. The trade discount is a reduction of the price and doesn't in any way depend on the time of payment. You see, in many trades the retail price of the goods is fixed by the manufacturer to make sure that they are sold everywhere at the same price. The goods are invoiced at this price and the retailer is allowed a trade discount which actually is his profit. In other cases the trade discount is used to give preferential treatment to certain types of customers, for example to wholesalers or exporters, to encourage them to give bulk orders. Often it is used to try to get bigger orders or to increase business at slack times. We sent a circular out last June and informed our customers that we would allow a trade discount of 5% on all orders received in July. It helped to keep our sales up that month and cleared a lot of old stock. One other important use of the trade discount is the adjustment of catalogue prices. Many firms—not Weavewell's, incidentally—issue yearly or half-yearly a comprehensive, often illustrated, catalogue in which the prices of all articles are shown. So you see if alterations in prices are necessary, they can be made by increasing or reducing the trade discount instead of reprinting the very expensive catalogue.

OLAF: Yes, I see that now. To come to another point; what happens if, in answer to an inquiry, you send out several patterns and then when you get the order you find we have no stock of one or two of them?

MR. AUSTIN: Of course, that happens very frequently. But you must remember that the price lists which we are sending out are not binding for us; they are not 'firm offers'. They are subject to two conditions: that the goods are unsold and that the prices have not changed in the meantime. Our customers know that, and if in a special case they want us to give a 'firm offer', they must state that in their inquiry. But if we make a firm offer we always limit it to one week by marking the price list: 'For acceptance within 7 days', because we cannot reserve the goods for a longer time and we must protect ourselves against a rise in prices.

If we get an order on a normal quotation and find that some articles have been sold out meantime, we either send the customer some similar patterns to choose from or select suitable substitutes which we send him 'on approval'. That means the customer has the right to return them if he does not like them. The main thing is, as always, not to lose a sale if you can possibly avoid it.

'... the customer has a right to return the goods
if he is not satisfied'

OLAF: That brings me to another question I wanted to ask you. What can you do to increase your sales or, as you say, your 'turnover'?

MR. AUSTIN: Well, if you watch me you'll see how I am trying to do it: by giving the customer prompt, courteous and reliable service and by understanding his wishes, his needs, and his difficulties. That is, I think, the best 'sales promotion'. There are, of course, many other things as well: personal visits, representatives and agents, advertisements and circulars . . . oh, there is quite a lot you can do. But first of all, you must not lose a 'prospect', that is, an order from a customer who has shown by an inquiry that he is interested in your goods.

OLAF: How can you make sure of that?

MR. AUSTIN: Well, we keep a copy of every price list or offer we send out. When an order is given, it is marked on the copy. The pattern clerk goes through these copies every week and where no order has been received he lets me know and I 'follow them up' by writing a friendly letter to the firm concerned. Some companies send a printed letter, but we feel that the personal approach is much more likely to be successful. If that does not do the trick,[1] I usually inform our representative and ask him to call.

OLAF: What is the difference between a representative and an agent?

MR. AUSTIN: The representative is an employee of the firm; he gets his salary, his expenses, and a small commission on his sales (we pay 1 %). He works only for our firm and has to carry out our instructions. The agent, on the other hand, relies mainly on his commission which is, of course, much higher. He works for several firms and is therefore much more independent. In the home trade we have only representatives, but overseas we employ a number of agents.

The greater part of our orders comes from 'reps' and agents and it is most important to keep them well informed of everything that is going on in their area. I hold regular conferences with them, listen to their complaints and their suggestions, and develop my plans and ideas for the coming season. That time is well spent because the 'reps' are the backbone of our sales organisation.

OLAF: Do you travel a lot yourself?

MR. AUSTIN: Well, sometimes I think I ought to travel more, but I simply haven't the time. Still, I manage to see the most important customers in London fairly regularly and those in the provinces once a year.

OLAF: And what about advertising? I noticed a few of your advertisements in the trade papers.

---

[1] *do the trick* = prove successful.

MR. AUSTIN: We don't actually advertise very much but we must, of course, keep our name continually before our customers' eyes and—what is more important—try to attract and interest new customers. In our trade, I think, the direct approach is more effective: we send out catalogues, price lists, showcards and material for window display, and if they go to the right people at the right time they always bring in plenty of orders and inquiries. And then, we often have something special to offer and customers are always interested in that.

I am just about to draft a circular for a special offer. We have bought the entire stock of a well-known Scottish factory, MacKiltie, at very low prices and I want to clear it quickly. The Christmas business is over but it will be very useful to many of our customers for their January sales. Would you like to try your hand at drafting the letter?

OLAF: I should like to very much, though I'll probably make a mess of it.

MR. AUSTIN: Well, let me just give you the points we want to make. MacKiltie's name is well known; that should be a very good selling point. Most people will know what they make but we'd better put it in: Tweeds,[1] Cheviots,[1] Donegals,[1] all pure wool. Everything is in stock but supplies are limited. Then we must mention the coming sales and finally ask them to write for samples or to visit our warehouse.

Well, see what you can do by tomorrow.

Exercises

I WORD STUDY. *Use each of the following:*

substitute ['sʌbstitjuːt] (noun and verb; use also *substitution* [sʌbsti'tjuːʃn]. How does this differ from *substitute*?), preferential (use also *prefer*), slack, bind, accept (also *acceptance*), instruction, prompt, courteous (also *courtesy*), trick ('to do the trick'), area, provinces (use also *provincial*).

[1] Types of cloth.

SOME EXPLANATIONS. SALES PROMOTION

II *Answer the following:*

1. What are 'terms'? 2. Explain: 30 days 5%, 60 days 2½%, 90 days net. 3. What is a trade discount? What is it used for? 4. Explain 'firm offers'. 5. On what condition are goods usually offered on a price list? 6. If you made a firm offer on a price list what phrase would you mark on it? 7. Why would you do this? 8. If you got an order on a normal quotation and found that some articles had been sold out meanwhile, what would you do? 9. Explain 'on approval'. 10. What can a Sales Manager do to increase turnover? 11. What is a 'prospect'? 12. What is the difference between a representative and an agent? 13. What is 'commission'? 14. Which is the more: 2½% of £10,000 or 5% of £5,000? 15. What would you do if you were told to 'use the direct approach' to your customers?

III *A prospective customer has written to your firm asking for your price list and enquiring about a special quality of an article that you manufacture. As he hasn't replied to your offer, you decide to send a 'follow-up letter'. Write the letter.*

IV *Try your hand at drafting the letter that Olaf has to take to Mr. Austin tomorrow.*

18
A Circular and the Inquiries from it

market price   on request   avail oneself of

Olaf brought his draft to Mr. Austin next day. When Mr. Austin had made a few alterations it read like this:

Weavewell Woollen Co. Ltd.
Victoria Street,
London, EC4X ISH

DA/LR   10th December, 19—.

Dear Sirs,
  We think that you will be interested to know that we have recently bought the entire stock of MacKiltie's Mills, Peebles, who, as you know, are renowned for their
  Scotch Tweeds, Cheviots and Donegals.
  We are in a position to offer these famous pure woollen qualities considerably below market price, and they should provide a very attractive line for your forthcoming sales.
  Orders can be supplied from stock but only limited quantities are available and when sold out cannot be repeated. The goods can be inspected at our warehouse or we shall be pleased to send patterns on request.
  We would strongly advise you to avail yourself of this exceptional opportunity.

                    Yours faithfully,
              p.p. Weavewell Woollen Co. Ltd.
                    D. AUSTIN
                    Sales Manager

MR. AUSTIN: We'll send it to all our town and country customers; we have not got enough to offer it for export. But I think this is a good opportunity to try to get some new customers. Look here, this is my index of firms with whom we should like to open an account. These cards are, of course, additional to our regular mailing list. Well, ask a girl to make you a stencil, run them off on the machine and see that they go out today.

It is the first big job which Olaf has done entirely by himself and he feels a kind of satisfaction when all the hundreds of letters are safely in the post by 6 o'clock.

Within a few days the results begin to show and inquiries are coming in. Here are some of them:

Postcard

Derby.
12th December, 19—.

Please send us patterns of Tweeds and Cheviots as mentioned in your circular.

Yours faithfully,
HENRY LUCAS & SON

Postcard

London Road,
Leicester.
12th December, 19—.

Thank you for your letter. Kindly send me samples with your lowest prices.

Yours faithfully,
T. R. BANKS

CHAPTER 18

Postcard

Northampton, 13th Dec., 19—.

We are interested in the MacKiltie qualities. When sending us patterns please show the available quantities in your price list.

Yours faithfully,
WALLIS & BURTON LTD.

Letter

Soames & Parsons
Rose Street,
Glasgow, G2 4WB

GS/LF 12th December, 19—.
Weavewell Woollen Co. Ltd.,
Victoria Street,
London, EC4X 1SH

Dear Sirs,

We thank you for your letter of 10th December with a special offer of Scotch Tweeds, etc., and should be pleased if you would send us patterns in grey and brown shades. If your terms are satisfactory we shall give you a good order.

Yours faithfully,
Soames & Parsons

G. SOAMES

As these inquiries are replies to an offer there is no need for another letter; they are passed to the pattern clerk who deals with them. But there is one inquiry in the post which comes from a very important new customer.

March and Spurling Ltd.
South Street,
Rugby, CV9 9AC

12th December, 19—.

Weavewell Woollen Co. Ltd.,
Victoria Street,
London, EC4X ISH

Dear Sirs,

We acknowledge with thanks your letter of 10th December. As we have always had an excellent sale for MacKiltie qualities, will you please send us a fairly comprehensive range of patterns.

Yours faithfully,
p.p. March & Spurling Ltd.
W. THOMAS

Mr. Austin wants to make quite sure of getting this order and so he writes to the customer and Weavewell's representative:

Letter to the customer

Weavewell Woollen Co. Ltd.
Victoria Street,
London, EC4X ISH

DA/LR   13th December, 19—.

Messrs. March & Spurling Ltd.,
South Street,
Rugby, CV9 9AC

Dear Sirs,

We are much obliged for your letter of yesterday asking for samples of MacKiltie Tweeds and Cheviots.

DEC

As our representative, Mr. Amery, will be in Rugby next week we have informed him of your inquiry and asked him to call on you. He will be able to show you the complete range of all articles we have in stock and give you any information you may require.

We shall be pleased to receive your order and we assure you of our best attention.

Yours faithfully,
p.p. Weavewell Woollen Co. Ltd.

D. AUSTIN
Sales Manager

Letter to the representative

Weavewell Woollen Co. Ltd.
Victoria Street,
London, EC4X ISH

DA/LR 13th December, 19—.

Dear Mr. Amery,

I am pleased to tell you that we have had a letter from March & Spurling in Rugby.

They are very interested in the MacKiltie qualities; we sent them the complete range of patterns last week.

It is important, I think, that we try to open this account at last; I know how often you have tried before. I would suggest that you change your plan for next week slightly, and go to Rugby on Monday or Tuesday. You might get quite a substantial order and may interest them in some of our other lines at the same time.

I have written to them and enclose a copy of my letter.

Jackman & Co., Leominster, wrote for samples of 'Specia' which is out of stock. We have offered the new quality 'Spectre' instead and have announced your visit. (Copy enclosed.)

We had a note from Reynold & Harvey, Coventry, asking for samples. They referred to our advertisement, but I am sure they remembered the firm from the various calls you and I have made there. Another proof of the truth of the saying: 'If at first you don't succeed . . .'[1] Unfortunately, I could not contact you that day, so in order not to waste time I sent them a very good offer from here (see copy). You may be able to look in on your way back from Rugby and see whether they have found what they wanted. They may be interested in our MacKiltie offer too. Try to get an order.

Yours sincerely,

Encl. D. AUSTIN

Exercises

I WORD STUDY. *Use the following:*

renowned, forthcoming, inspect (also *inspection*), comprehensive, range, contact (verb and noun).

II *Use these phrases in sentences of your own:*

1. are renowned for; 2. considerably below market price; 3. a very attractive line; 4. your forthcoming sales; 5. only limited quantities are available; 6. we would strongly advise you; 7. mentioned in your circular; 8. a fairly comprehensive range; 9. open this account; 10. in order not to waste time; 11. avail yourself of this opportunity.

[1] If at first you don't succeed, try, try, try again (*proverb*).

III 1. The firm of Grafton & Co. have obtained a large quantity of Brazilian coffee at very favourable prices. Draft a circular letter to their customers.

2. Write a letter from your firm (wholesale coal merchants) to a retailer, offering coal at unusually low prices. Make quite clear that the low price doesn't mean poor quality.

3. The firm (wholesale soap manufacturers) of which you are sales manager has had inquiries from an important retailer in Birmingham. Write a letter to your representative for that district instructing him to call.

19
Orders and their Execution

order form   order number   credit control   despatch   bale
goods train   passenger train   concession   financial standing
repeat order   advance order   market   order book   copy order
confirmation   in due course

In the preceding chapters we have seen how inquiries arrive every day, how they are dealt with, how offers and patterns, price lists and circulars are sent out. All this is done with one purpose: to obtain orders.

Every quotation does not, of course, result in an order, but if inquiries are handled with experience and skill the customer will in many cases be interested in some of the articles offered and will place an order.

Some orders simply take the form of a postcard or a short letter like the following:

S. G. Hamilton & Co.
64, Newgate Street,
Southport, PR8 1DH

12th December, 19—.

Weavewell Woollen Co. Ltd.,
Victoria Street,
London, EC4X 1SH

Dear Sirs,
In reply to your letter of 9th December with price list, for which we thank you, will you please send us by return
2 pieces 8008   1 piece 9010

Your immediate attention will oblige.

> Yours faithfully,
> For S. G. Hamilton & Co.
> *S. LLOYD*

Most orders, however, come on printed order forms, sometimes accompanied by a letter if a customer wants to stress a special point. There is an obvious advantage in the use of a standardised order form. All the necessary instructions are printed and no important point can be forgotten. A glance at the orders below will show that there are special columns for quantities, articles, prices, delivery dates, which have to be filled in. Space is provided for terms, method of transport, marks (where necessary) and last but not least for the order number (O/N). This number is important: it has to be quoted on every invoice, and on all correspondence relating to the order. This provides the customer with an easy reference to his order and enables him to check deliveries against his orders and to keep his order book up-to-date.

After an order has been received, it is first checked to see whether it is correct and whether it agrees with the original quotation. When that has been done it goes through the credit control; in most cases the Sales Manager knows whether the customer is good for the amount in question and marks it accordingly. Where he is doubtful he will refer to the Accounts Department. If the order is for future delivery, it is entered into the order books of the firm; orders which can be executed from stock are passed to the warehouse (see pages 138-9).

In many cases, however, some difficulty or other may arise: goods may be out of stock, a customer may ask for special terms or for extension of credit, delivery dates may have to be adjusted or references to be taken up in the case of a new customer. In all these cases special correspondence is necessary and the execution of the order may be held up until these points have been cleared.

Here are a few examples:

a) An order is received and one of the articles ordered is out of stock:

R. L. Street & Co. Ltd.
156, North Street,
Chester, CH2 1GS

12th December, 19—.

Weavewell Woollen Co. Ltd.,
Victoria Street,
London, EC4X 1SH

Dear Sirs,

    We thank you for your letter of 9th December (your ref. DA/LR) with patterns and price list.

    We have selected four qualities and have pleasure in enclosing our order No. 1025 for your attention.

    As the goods are urgently required, may we ask you to despatch them without delay.

                      Yours faithfully,
                      For R. L. Street & Co. Ltd.
                      P. HARRIS

Encl. Order No. 1025.

The actual order is given on the next page.

R. L. Street & Co. Ltd.
156, North Street,
Chester, CH2 1GS

12th December, 19—.

Order No. 1025
(please quote on all invoices).
Weavewell Woollen Co. Ltd.,
Victoria Street,
London, EC4X 1SH

Dear Sirs,
   Please supply:

Quantity	Article	Price	Delivery
16 yds.	9009	£1.91	prompt
16 ,,	7642	£1.75	,,
16 ,,	8344	£1.89	,,
16 ,,	2428	£1.84	,,

Despatch by Passenger Train.

                              30 days/$2\frac{1}{2}$%.

                        For R. L. Street & Co. Ltd.
                        P. HARRIS

When this order is checked it is found that one article is out of stock. As the customer expressly states that the goods are urgently needed, Mr. Austin decides to substitute a similar material and writes the following letter:

Weavewell Woollen Co. Ltd.
Victoria Street,
London, EC4X 1SH

DA/LR
13th December, 19—.

Messrs. R. L. Street & Co. Ltd.,
156, North Street,
Chester, CH2 1GS

Dear Sirs,

Your Order No. 1025

    We acknowledge with thanks your letter of 12th December and are pleased to see that some of the articles we offered you have met with your approval.

    An extremely large order for 8344 has unexpectedly exhausted our stocks of this material and, as you asked for immediate delivery, we have substituted our quality 8347 at the same price. This cloth has only just come into stock and we think it is most attractive and certainly excellent value for money.

    The goods are being despatched today by passenger train and should reach you tomorrow. We trust that they will be to your satisfaction and hope to receive further orders from you in the future.

                      Yours faithfully,
                p.p. Weavewell Woollen Co. Ltd.
                    D. AUSTIN
                    Sales Manager

b) The next order comes from Brown & Carter, Liverpool, with a letter asking for a trade discount of 5% instead of 2½% as offered.

Brown & Carter Ltd.
Ushfield House,
Liverpool, L3 3TC

11th December, 19—.

Weavewell Woollen Co. Ltd.,
Victoria Street,
London, EC4X 1SH

Dear Sirs,

Exp. 4022

We acknowledge the receipt of your letter of 9th December and have submitted the gaberdines, of which you sent us samples, to our customer.

We have obtained an order for 7 pieces but on the condition that a trade discount of 5% must be given. We are most anxious to build up our export connections and hope that you will assist us in our efforts. Enclosed please find our order form No. 6143. If you can accept the terms offered by our customer we would ask you to arrange for immediate delivery.

Your reply by return will oblige.

Yours faithfully,
For Brown & Carter Ltd.
H. GRIGSON

HG/RS
Encl.

Brown & Carter Ltd.
Ushfield House,
Liverpool, L3 3TC

11th December, 19—.

Order Form No. 6143/Exp. 4022
(Please quote.)
Weavewell Woollen Co. Ltd.,
Victoria Street,
London, EC4X 1SH

Dear Sirs,

    Please supply as specified below:

Description	Quantity	Price	Delivery
Gab. 4	3 pieces	£1.35 less 5%	prompt
,, 101	2 ,,	£1.08 ,, 5%	,,
,, 115	2 ,,	£0.99 ,, 5%	,,

Bales to
be marked: By Goods Train   30/2½%
  B C
   L

                        For Brown & Carter Ltd.
                          H. GRIGSON

In this case Mr. Austin decides to allow the increased trade discount and sends the following answer:

Weavewell Woollen Co. Ltd.
Victoria Street,
London, EC4X ISH

DA/LR 12th December, 19—.
Messrs. Brown & Carter Ltd.,
Ushfield House,
Liverpool, L3 3TC.

Dear Sirs,

Export 4022, Order No. 6143

We thank you for your letter of 11th December with order No. 6143 for 7 pieces gaberdine.

Although our prices do not really allow any concession we have in this case decided to accept your order and to grant you a trade discount of 5%. We do this because we want to assist you in extending your exports and in the hope that this will lead to repeat orders.

The goods will be put on rail tomorrow and our invoice will follow in due course.

                    Yours faithfully,
            p.p. Weavewell Woollen Co. Ltd.

              D. AUSTIN
              Sales Manager

---

c) The same day Murphy & Hale of Exeter send an order for 5 pieces 'Elasto' but write that the delivery dates on the quotation do not satisfy them.

Murphy & Hale Ltd.
16, Barnstaple Road,
Exeter, EX3 6NH

11th December, 19—.

Weavewell Woollen Co. Ltd.,
Victoria Street,
London, EC4X 1SH

Dear Sirs,

With reference to your letter of 10th December we note that you are not in a position to allow us the special discount we asked for.

We have decided, however, to give you a standing order for your quality 'Elasto' and enclose our order form No. 1649. As we want to avoid being out of stock of this article, we must ask you to supply one piece in January and one piece in February. As this is in your interest as well as in ours we hope that you will try to assist us in this matter.

Awaiting your reply,

     We are,

          Yours faithfully,
          Murphy & Hale Ltd.

          ALLAN HALE
          Director

AH/P
Encl.

The order form is shown overleaf.

CHAPTER 19

Murphy & Hale Ltd.
**16, Barnstaple Road,
Exeter, EX3 6NH**

11th December, 19—.

Please quote No. 1649
Weavewell Woollen Co. Ltd.,
Victoria Street,
London, EC4X 1SH

Dear Sirs,

Please supply the undermentioned goods:

Description	Quantity	Price	Delivery
Elasto	1	£1.89	January
,,	1	,,	February
,,	2	,,	March
,,	2	,,	April
,,	1	,,	May

By rail   30 days 2½%

Murphy & Hale Ltd.
ALLAN HALE
Director

Again Mr. Austin decides to agree to the customer's request and replies as follows:

Weavewell Woollen Co. Ltd.
Victoria Street,
London, EC4X 1SH

DA/LR
Messrs. Murphy & Hale Ltd.,
16, Barnstaple Road,
Exeter, EX3 6NH

13th December, 19—.

Dear Sirs,

Your Order No. 1649

We acknowledge with thanks your letter of 11th December with order No. 1649, which has had our attention.

We are pleased that you have decided to stock our quality 'Elasto' regularly and we are confident that the sales will satisfy you in every respect.

As we pointed out in our letter of 10th December our orders for this quality are very heavy, but we have arranged to supply you with one piece in January and one in February. We confirm accordingly that we shall supply 7 pieces 'Elasto' @[1] £1.89 (1 January, 1 February, 2 March, 2 April, 1 May).

It will help us to supply you promptly if for orders of this quality you can let us have about three months' advance notice. We look forward to receiving your further orders.

> Yours faithfully,
> p.p. Weavewell Woollen Co. Ltd.
> *D. AUSTIN*
> Sales Manager

---

[1] @ = at.

d) An order is received from Soames & Parsons, Glasgow, asking for an extension of credit:

Soames & Parsons
Rose Street,
Glasgow, G2 4WB

GS/LF   15th December, 19—.

Weavewell Woollen Co. Ltd.,
Victoria Street,
London, EC4X 1SH

Dear Sirs,

    We thank you for your offer of 13th December. The prices and qualities appear to be satisfactory and we enclose an order for your attention.

    As business is rather slack at the moment we must ask you to alter your terms slightly and to allow us payment in 60 days with $2\frac{1}{2}\%$. Delivery is required on 5th January.

    Kindly inform us by return whether you can book the order on these terms.

                                                Yours faithfully,
                                                Soames & Parsons

                                                G. SOAMES

Encl.

No Sales Manager worth his salt[1] will refuse an order because of a slight extension of terms. On the other hand, Mr. Austin wants to make it quite clear that he is making an exception and points this out in his reply.

[1] *Worth his salt* = doing his job properly.

Weavewell Woollen Co. Ltd.
**Victoria Street,
London, EC4X ISH**

DA/LR   17th December, 19—.

Messrs. Soames & Parsons,
Rose Street,
Glasgow, G2 4WB.

Dear Sirs,

    We are in receipt of your letter of 15th December and thank you for your order No. 2573 which we have accepted on the terms you propose. From the many years we have done business together you know that we always try to meet the reasonable wishes of our customers. We must ask you, however, to realise that this concession is exceptional and that future orders can be executed only on our normal trade terms.

    Enclosed please find our official confirmation.

    We shall be pleased to receive your further orders, which shall have our most careful attention.

                    Your faithfully,
                p.p. Weavewell Woollen Co. Ltd.
                    D. AUSTIN
                    Sales Manager

Encl.

e) Order from a new customer giving references:

John Sterling & Co.
Market Place,
Norwich, NOR1 5JC

Our Ref.   Your Ref.
HS/FK   DA/LR   11th December, 19—.
Weavewell Woollen Co. Ltd.,
Victoria Street,
London, EC4X 1SH

Dear Sirs,

    We are in receipt of your letter of 5th December and the pattern book of your 'Goldring' qualities.

It seems that there should be a market for this article in Norwich and we have therefore decided to place a trial order for which we enclose our official order form No. 1647.

Regarding our financial standing we would refer you to the following firms:

Messrs. Simpson & West Ltd., Bradford.
Messrs. Slater & Steel Ltd., Fore St., London, E.C.2.

    We are awaiting your early reply.

                              Yours faithfully,
                          For John Sterling & Co.
                            H. STREET

John Sterling & Co.
**Market Place,
Norwich, NOR1 5JC**

11th December, 19—.

No. 1647
(Please quote on Invoice.)
Weavewell Woollen Co. Ltd.,
Victoria Street,
London, EC4X 1SH

Dear Sirs,
   Please deliver at the prices, terms and dates as given below:

Quantity	Quality	Price	Date
25/27 yds.	Goldring II	£1.42	Jan./Feb.
25/27 ,,	,, III	£1.48	,,
1 piece	,, IX	£1.36	,,
2 pieces	,, X	£1.51	,,
Marks: J S			30/2½%
N	By Goods Train		60/net

Weavewell Woollen Co. Ltd.
**Victoria Street,
London, EC4X 1SH**

DA/LR   15th December, 19—.
Messrs. John Sterling & Co.,
Market Place,
Norwich, NOR1 5JC

Dear Sirs,
   With reference to your letter of 11th December we thank you for your order No. 1647 for delivery Jan./Feb., 19—.

We have taken up the references[1] which you have kindly supplied and now have pleasure in enclosing our illustrated[2] copy order which we trust you will find correct.

We hope that this order will give you full satisfaction and that it will lead to a pleasant and lasting connection between our houses.[3] Please be assured that we shall endeavour to assist you in every way.

Yours faithfully,
p.p. Weavewell Woollen Co. Ltd.,

D. AUSTIN
Sales Manager

Encl.

COPY ORDER

Weavewell Woollen Co. Ltd.
Victoria Street,
London, EC4X ISH

15th December, 19--.

Messrs. John Sterling & Co., Market Place, Norwic

We thank you for your order of 11th Dec. which we confirm herewith as follows (1647)

Delivery: Jan./Feb. Terms: 30 days 2½%. 60 days ne

Marks: J S
        N   By Goods Train.

Quality	Colours	Quantity	Price
Goldring	11	25/7	£1.42
"	111	25/7	£1.48
"	1 X	1 piece	£1.36
"	X	2 pieces	£1.51

[1] See pp. 176-7.
[2] *Illustrated* here means that a pattern of each quality ordered is sent with the confirmation.
[3] *House* here means 'business house' or 'firm'. This use is becoming a little old-fashioned.

'... a pleasant and lasting connection between our houses'

f) Naturally, some of the letters that come in are disappointing; here is a letter from Reynold & Harvey, Coventry, who write that they could not give an order because they considered the offer they had from their regular supplier more attractive. Fortunately, in this case Mr. Austin had already instructed his representative to call on the customer and there is still hope that his personal effort will have the desired result. Mr. Austin explains that very many firms are unwilling to open new accounts just because they don't like making a change. He writes to Reynold & Harvey and sends a copy to his representative; let us take the customer's letter first:

Reynold & Harvey
14, King Street,
Coventry, CV5 4MB

JR/HG 13th December, 19—.
Weavewell Woollen Co. Ltd.,
Victoria Street,
London, EC4X 1SH

Dear Sirs,

We thank you for your letter of 10th December with enclosures.

After comparing your offer carefully with that of our regular supplier, we found his quotation more favourable and are therefore unable to place an order with you.

We are returning your samples herewith.

Yours faithfully,
Reynold & Harvey

J. REYNOLD

Encl.

Here is Mr. Austin's reply:

Weavewell Woollen Co. Ltd.
Victoria Street,
London, EC4X 1SH

DA/LR 14th December, 19—.
Messrs. Reynold & Harvey,
14, King Street,
Coventry, CV5 4MB

Dear Sirs,

We are very sorry indeed to see from your letter of 13th

December that you did not find our offer interesting enough to give us an order.

You will appreciate that an offer by post can only represent a very limited selection from our wide range. We have, however, informed our representative for Coventry, Mr. Amery, of your inquiry and he will most probably call on you within the next few days. We should be much obliged if you would let him show you our complete collection; we are hoping that you will find several articles that are suitable for you.

We have just bought the entire stock of MacKiltie's Mills and can offer these famous qualities at very advantageous prices. Mr. Amery will be pleased to show you these and we feel sure that they will interest you.

Yours faithfully,
p.p. Weavewell Woollen Co. Ltd.
D. AUSTIN
Sales Manager

Exercises

I WORD STUDY. *Use the following:*

preceding (use also *precede* and *proceed*), glance, column, transport, quote, provide, arise (give the parts of this verb), adjust, reference (note the two meanings as shown in the phrases 'to take up references', 'with reference to your letter'), submit (note two meanings and constructions):

1. The people had *to submit to* the rule of the conqueror (i.e. had to surrender to, to yield to).
2. We have *submitted* the cloth to our customer (i.e. have put it before him or sent it to him for his consideration). Note also '*submit* an offer'.

specify (also *specification*), assist (also *assistance* and *assistant*), undermentioned, confirm (and *confirmation*), market (note the various uses as noun and verb, e.g.):

1. A *market* is held here every week.
2. There should be a *market* for these goods in Norwich; they will easily *find a market*.
3. As the *market* is at present, it is difficult to sell these goods.
4. We are selling these below *market* price.
5. The firm will *market* (i.e. sell) the goods.

endeavour, appreciate (note three meanings):
1. You will *appreciate* that an offer by post can only represent a limited selection (=quite understand).
2. I *appreciate* your kindness in this matter (=set a high value on, feel grateful for. See page 74).
3. The goods have *appreciated* in value (=increased).

II *Punctuate and arrange correctly:*

a. 54 croydon rd epsom surrey 8 december 19— messrs brown and robinson st pauls st london e c 4 dear sirs we thank you for your quotation of 2nd december and should be glad to receive 200 of your 'Newstyle' fountain pens at 40p as we want to show these in time for the christmas trade it is important that we should have immediate delivery if you cannot let us have the goods here within three days please cancel the order we hope you can oblige us in this matter and we hope to be able to place further orders with you yours faithfully pp. david green and son p tate sales manager.

b. jackson shaw and co ltd hesketh works ormskirk lancashire 15th may 19— messrs henry walton and co ltd warrington dear sirs in answer to your inquiry for oil cakes for cattle we can offer the following from our present stock east african cake or meal £9.88 per ton brazilian oilcake £10.24 per ton canadian oilcake £11.13 per ton we are sending you a sample of each quality by parcel post terms 30 days 5% 60 days $2\frac{1}{2}$% 3 months net yours faithfully per pro jackson shaw and co ltd t s jackson director.

III *Note carefully the following phrases from letters in Chapter 19 and use each of them in sentences of your own:*

1. enclosing our order No. 1025; 2. urgently required; 3. immediate despatch; 4. please quote; 5. meet with your approval; 6. substituted our cloth 8347; 7. by passenger train;

ORDERS AND THEIR EXECUTION

8. submitted them to our customer; 9. on the condition that a trade discount is given; 10. enclosed please find; 11. as specified below; 12. by goods train; 13. allow any concession; 14. grant you a trade discount; 15. will lead to repeat orders; 16. put on rail tomorrow; 17. will follow in due course; 18. are not in a position to allow; 19. to give you a standing order; 20. being out of stock of this article; 21. is in your interest; 22. the undermentioned goods; 23. we confirm accordingly; 24. appear to be satisfactory; 25. kindly inform us by return; 26. in receipt of your letter; 27. on the terms you propose; 28. this concession is exceptional; 29. future orders can be executed only; 30. normal trade terms.

IV *Explain:* order form, order number, order book, repeat order, standing order, trial order, advance order, copy order.

V *Write the following letters:*

1. Acknowledge a quotation but regret you are not able to place an order.
2. Messrs. Russell and Matthews of Bristol will place an order for 10,000 tins of fruit at the price quoted if they are given a trade discount of $7\frac{1}{2}\%$. Write their letter and the reply either allowing the discount or refusing it.
3. Place an order for 1,000 bags of cement that you need urgently. Make this fact quite clear and give instructions about transport.
4. Messrs. Newman & Turner have replied unfavourably to your circular letter about men's shirts saying that their present supplier has more varied stock at cheaper prices. Write a reply.
5. You want to place a first order for 300 men's hats with the Luton Headwear Co. Write a letter to accompany the order giving references. Send the reply of the Luton Headwear Co.
6. Messrs. Whittard & Co. of Bond St. send an order form ordering five different qualities of tea to the International Tea Co., Mincing Lane, London. Write out the order forms and the accompanying letter. Also write a reply from the International Tea Co. regretting that one of the qualities of tea ordered is at the moment out of stock but saying that they have substituted another.

20
Complaints, Apologies and Adjustments

**contract   carriage forward   carriage paid   Credit Note
on sale or return   clerical error**

But of all the letters Mr. Austin has to deal with one type is the most difficult and delicate: letters which contain a complaint. In spite of every possible care and attention that is given to the customers' wishes and orders, such letters will arrive. There are various reasons: delays are often unavoidable, customers find some fault with the goods supplied, a mistake may have crept in; in fact the sources of complaints seem inexhaustible.

As a rule, however, a customer will not complain unless he thinks he has good reason; and when he complains he expects his supplier to put the matter right. One wrong word, any lack of tact on the part of the supplier may mean the loss of a valuable customer; and a customer who thinks he has not had a fair deal will not easily forget his grievance. The Sales Manager must distinguish between genuine complaints and those without foundation. Where he is in doubt he should act on the principle, 'the customer is always right'. In dealing with a complaint the Sales Manager will generally begin his letter with an expression of regret, explain the circumstances that have caused the complaint to be made, and suggest some settlement that, it is hoped, will meet the complaint. Above all, both in writing letters of complaint and in answering them the keynote should always be COURTESY.

Complaints may be grouped under four main headings:
(a) delay,
(b) quality,
(c) price,
(d) error.

'... a customer will not complain unless he thinks he has good reason'

a) Complaints concerning delays

A. Penny & Co. Ltd.
60, Market Place,
Portsmouth, PO1 9MJ

16th March, 19—.

Weavewell Woollen Co. Ltd.,
Victoria Street,
London, EC4X 1SH

Dear Sirs,

Our Order No. 697

On 4th September we ordered 16 pieces of Saxony cloth for delivery mid-February. As the goods have not yet arrived, we must ask you to despatch them without further delay. Unless the goods are received within 10 days we shall have to cancel our order.

>Awaiting your reply,
>We are,
>Yours faithfully,
>For A. Penny & Co. Ltd.
>S. DUNN

Reply

Weavewell Woollen Co. Ltd.
Victoria Street,
London, EC4X 1SH

DA/LR   17th March, 19—.

Messrs. A. Penny & Co. Ltd.,
60, Market Place,
Portsmouth, PO1 9MJ

Dear Sirs,

Your Order No. 697

We have your letter of 16th March and regret very much that we have not yet been able to execute your order No. **697** of 4th September. We are, of course, aware that these pieces are long overdue, but work at the factory was held up for several weeks through shortage of raw material. We have, however, been informed that we shall probably have delivery within the next few days and we have instructed the factory to despatch the goods to you direct in order to save time.

We assure you that we are doing our best to speed up delivery and we offer our apologies for the inconvenience the delay has caused you.

Yours faithfully,
p.p. Weavewell Woollen Co. Ltd.
D. AUSTIN
Sales Manager

D. Moore & Sons Ltd.
Gloucester, GL1 1EG

21st October, 19—.

Weavewell Woollen Co. Ltd.,
Victoria Street, London, EC4X 1SH

Dear Sirs,

Our Order No. 364

On 30th September we reminded you that our order of 3rd August was for delivery on 15th September and that unless it was despatched by return we would have to withdraw from the contract.

As these goods were required for the Autumn season, we now have no use for them and must therefore ask you to cancel our order.

Yours faithfully,
D. Moore & Sons Ltd.
D. MOORE

CHAPTER 20

Reply

Weavewell Woollen Co. Ltd.
Victoria Street,
London, EC4X 1SH

DA/LR   23rd October, 19—.

Messrs. D. Moore & Sons Ltd.,
Gloucester, GL1 1EG

Dear Sirs,

Your Order No. 364

We acknowledge the receipt of your letter of 21st October and are extremely sorry that causes completely beyond our control have made it impossible for us to keep the delivery date of 15th September. The recent railway strike held up supplies of coal and raw material and resulted in delays of 6 to 10 weeks. We have made every possible effort to speed up delivery but unfortunately without success.

In the circumstances we have no alternative but to accept your cancellation with regret, but we would ask you to believe that the delay was in no way caused by any negligence on our part.

Whilst offering our sincere apologies we trust that you will understand the position and that you will continue to place your orders with us.

                              Yours faithfully,
                     p.p. Weavewell Woollen Co. Ltd.

                              D. AUSTIN
                              Sales Manager

b) Complaints concerning quality

F. R. Beach & Sons
Stockport, SK1 7PL

10th November, 19—.

Weavewell Woollen Co. Ltd.,
Victoria Street,
London, EC4X 1SH.

Dear Sirs,

Order No. 3124. Your invoice No. 86342

We have today received the three pieces Bouclé[1] which we ordered on 2nd October.

On examination we find that two pieces do not correspond with the original pattern, as the colour is much paler. This gives them a greyish shade which looks most unattractive. We still have half a piece of your September delivery in stock and we want to use this with the new pieces, but the difference in colour makes this quite impossible.

We are therefore returning the pieces to you, carriage forward,[2] and would ask you to send us your Credit Note.

Yours faithfully,
F. R. Beach & Sons
L. BEACH

---

[1] Type of cloth.
[2] Carriage forward (see footnote, page 148).

Reply

Weavewell Woollen Co. Ltd.
Victoria Street,
London, EC4X 1SH

DA/LR 15th November, 19—.

Messrs. F. R. Beach & Sons,
Stockport, SK1 7PL

Dear Sirs,

Your Order No. 3124

We very much regret to learn from your letter of 10th November, 19—, that two pieces of our delivery of 1st November were unsatisfactory.

While slight differences in colour are unavoidable, we appreciate your problem in matching the pieces with part of our previous delivery and shall, of course, take the two pieces back. We are expecting new deliveries next week and shall then carefully select two pieces which are completely identical with the original.

We hope that this will meet your wishes and we apologise for the inconvenience you have been caused.

Yours faithfully,
p.p. Weavewell Woollen Co. Ltd.

D. AUSTIN
Sales Manager

Then there are complaints because of increases in price. **Here** is an example:

c) Complaints concerning price

Henry Lee & Co. Ltd.
Petersfield, GU6 2TC

16th November, 19—.

Weavewell Woollen Co. Ltd.,
Victoria Street,
London, EC4X 1SH

Dear Sirs,

Our Order 646

Last March we had from you one piece 'Elasto' at £1.80 per yard. On 8th October we sent you a repeat order (our order No. 646) and are surprised to see from your invoice, received today, that you are now charging £1.89 per yard.

Though we realise that prices have gone up slightly since March, an increase of over 5% seems to us out of all proportion.

We must ask you to let us have a substantial reduction or, failing this, to let us return this piece to you.

Yours faithfully,
For Henry Lee & Co. Ltd.

C. S. JOHNSON

This kind of complaint calls for a very cautious reply, but Mr. Austin has learned from the experience of many years how to deal with it without annoying the customer.

EEC

Reply

Weavewell Woollen Co. Ltd.
Victoria Street,
London, EC4X 1SH

DA/LR
18th November, 19—.

Messrs. Henry Lee & Co. Ltd.,
Petersfield, GU6 2TC

Dear Sirs,

From your letter of 16th November, 19—, we see with regret that you consider the price of our quality 'Elasto' too high.

May we explain that there are two reasons for the apparently considerable increase: our prices in March were based on an old contract of which we gave our customers the full benefit; the correct price at that time should have been £1.84 to £1.86. At the same time as this contract came to an end we had to face the sudden rise in merino prices which, as you know, took place in September/October.

The price of £1.89 has been most carefully calculated and we regret we are quite unable to allow even the smallest reduction. As a matter of fact, we shall have to increase it by another 3p very shortly.

We admit that these frequent changes of price are most unfortunate, but, as the market is at present, they cannot be avoided. We hope that you will feel able to keep the piece in question, as we are confident that you will find a ready sale for this popular quality.

Yours truly,
p.p. Weavewell Woollen Co. Ltd.
D. AUSTIN
Sales Manager

COMPLAINTS, APOLOGIES AND ADJUSTMENTS

'... unable to allow even the smallest reduction'

---

d) Error

Brown & Carter Ltd.
Ushfield House,
Liverpool, L3 3TC

15th December, 19—.

Weavewell Woollen Co. Ltd.,
Victoria Street,
London, EC4X 1SH

Dear Sirs,

Our Order No. 6143/Exp. 4022

We have today received 2 bales containing 7 pieces gaberdine and find to our surprise that the bale $^{BC}_{L}$ 166 contains 2 pieces Gab. 110 instead of Gab. 101 as ordered.

This mistake is most unfortunate because, as you know, the goods are required for an export order which has to be shipped this week. Please wire or telephone us on receipt of this letter and let us know whether you can despatch 2 pieces Gab. 101 without fail tomorrow by passenger train.

In order to save the expense of returning the two wrong pieces to you we would be prepared to keep them 'on sale or return'. We think that we may be able to dispose of them and await your answer as to whether you agree to our proposal.

> Yours faithfully,
> For Brown & Carter Ltd.
> H. GRIGSON

HG/RS

Reply

Weavewell Woollen Co. Ltd.
Victoria Street,
London, EC4X 1SH

DA/LR
16th December, 19—.

Messrs. Brown & Carter Ltd.,
Ushfield House,
Liverpool, L3 3TC

Dear Sirs,

<u>*Order No. 6143/Exp. 4022*</u>

With reference to the telephone conversation we had with you today we want to repeat our sincere apologies for the most unfortunate error that has occurred in the execution of your order. We are completely at a loss to understand how this mistake could happen as all goods are checked and cross-checked at every stage before despatch. It is, we think, the first time in all these years that you have had cause to complain, and we shall take every care to avoid giving you any future cause of complaint.

The 2 pieces Gab. 101 were despatched today by the 12.30 train to Liverpool and will definitely be in your possession tomorrow morning. We are pleased to think that this will enable you to get the shipment out in time but we are very sorry indeed to have caused you so much trouble.

We much appreciate your willingness to retain the two pieces Gab. 110 'on sale or return'.[1] You know that as a rule we do not supply on this basis, but we shall make an exception in this case to compensate you to some extent for the inconvenience you have been caused. We have accordingly instructed our Invoice Department to charge the two pieces 'on sale or return' for 3 months and would ask you to let us have an account for them by the end of March.

We hope that the matter is thus settled to our mutual satisfaction, and remain,

                Yours faithfully,
          p.p. Weavewell Woollen Co. Ltd.

              D. AUSTIN
              Sales Manager

Brown & Carter Ltd.
Ushfield House,
Liverpool, L3 3TC

                              16th December, 19—.

Weavewell Woollen Co. Ltd.,
Victoria Street,
London, EC4X 1SH

Dear Sirs,

          Our Order No. 6143
          Your Inv. No. 86469

Further to our letter of yesterday we find on checking your invoice of 13th December that you have charged Gab. 4 at £1.45 instead of £1.35 as quoted by you on 9th December. We can only

---

[1] Goods supplied 'on sale or return' can be held by the customer for a specified period. At the end of this period he has to account for his sales and to pay for them; goods unsold can be returned.

assume that this is due to a clerical error. Our sale was, of course, based on the price of £1.35. Perhaps you will look into the matter and let us have a Credit Note for the difference in due course.

Yours faithfully,
For Brown & Carter Ltd.
H. GRIGSON

HG/RS

Reply

Weavewell Woollen Co. Ltd.
Victoria Street,
London, EC4X 1SH

DA/LR   17th December, 19—.
Messrs. Brown & Carter Ltd.,
Ushfield House,
Liverpool, L3 3TC.

Dear Sirs,

Order No. 6143/Exp. 4022

We hasten to reply to your letter of 16th December and to apologise for the regrettable mistake which you had to point out. It is most unfortunate that two errors should have occurred in the execution of your order and we need not tell you how sorry we are. The only excuse which we can offer is the extreme pressure under which we have been working and the illness of the head of our invoicing department. We enclose our Credit Note and express our sincere apologies for these mistakes.

Your orders will receive our most careful attention and we hope that you will have no further reasons for complaints.

>Yours faithfully,
>p.p. Weavewell Woollen Co. Ltd.
>*D. AUSTIN*
>Sales Manager

Encl. 1 C/N[1]

'... the extreme pressure under which we have been working'

---

[1] C/N = Credit Note (see page 154ff).

Exercises

I WORD STUDY. *Use the following:*

cancel (use also the noun *cancellation*), execute (and execution [eksə'kju:ʃən]. Note two meanings), aware, overdue, shortage, recent, alternative, neglect (also *negligence*), correspond (note two meanings), shade (in the letter on page 123 it means *colour*. What other meaning has it?), attractive (also *attract, attraction, unattractive*), avoid (also *avoidable, unavoidable*), select, identical (also *identity, identify*), apologise (also *apology* [ə'pɔlədʒi], *apologetic* [əpɔlə'dʒetik]), substantial, reduction (also *reduce*. What is the opposite?), apparent (also *apparently*), influence (noun and verb), confident, dispose (of) (note the meaning: 'get rid of', 'deal with'), error, check (noun with three meanings and verb with two. Compare with *cheque*), complain (also *complaint*), ship (noun and verb; use also *shipment*), appreciate, retain, compensate ['kɔmpenseit] (also *compensation* [kɔmpen'seiʃn]), wire[1] (verb).

II *Insert the missing prepositions or adverbs:*

1. Mr. Austin has to deal —— many letters.
2. Mistakes will occur —— spite —— all we can do.
3. They found fault —— the goods supplied.
4. A mistake —— the part —— the supplier may lose a customer.
5. You must distinguish —— complaints that are genuine and those that are not.
6. If you are —— doubt agree —— the customer.
7. In dealing —— a complaint, begin —— an expression —— regret.
8. We will send the goods —— further delay.
9. We shall do this —— order to save time.
10. We offer apologies —— the delay.
11. The goods ordered —— 3rd August were —— delivery —— 15th September.
12. The goods will be sent —— return —— post.
13. The causes —— the delay were —— our control.
14. —— the circumstances we have no alternative.
15. The delay was not caused —— any negligence —— our part.

[1] The terms *telegram* or *wire* are used for *inland* messages; *cable* is used for messages going abroad.

COMPLAINTS, APOLOGIES AND ADJUSTMENTS

16. We find —— examination that the pieces do not correspond —— the original pattern.
17. This piece is completely identical —— the original.
18. This price is —— —— all proportion.
19. We found —— our surprise cloth 110 —— —— cloth 101 as ordered.
20. Please telephone us —— receipt —— this letter.

III *Use these phrases in sentences of your own:*

1. We must ask you to despatch them; 2. work has been held up; 3. shortage of raw material; 4. we assure you; 5. we offer our apologies; 6. withdraw from the contract; 7. cancel our order; 8. causes completely beyond our control; 9. resulted in delays; 10. we have no alternative but; 11. any negligence on our part; 12. carriage forward; 13. we very much regret to learn; 14. apologise for the inconvenience; 15. seems to us out of all proportion; 16. when this contract came to an end; 17. we regret we are quite unable to; 18. as the market is at present; 19. in order to save the expense; 20. we should be prepared to; 21. we are completely at a loss to understand; 22. we shall take every care; 23. to our mutual satisfaction; 24. a clerical error; 25. a regrettable mistake; 26. in due course; 27. on checking your invoice; 28. we can only assume.

IV . *Write the following letters:*

1. A letter to a firm of pottery manufacturers complaining that in an order for cups and saucers and plates you find a number of second quality articles, though you ordered and were invoiced for first quality.
2. A reply from the pottery manufacturers apologising for the mistake in the packing department
3. A letter to the Coldstore Manufacturing Company complaining of delay in the despatch of 18 refrigerators ordered two months ago.
4. A letter of apology and explanation from Coldstore Manufacturing Co.
5. Letter to Silko Stocking Co. complaining that ladies' stockings sent 15th May were not the same quality as the sample pair shown by their representative.

6. Letter of explanation from Silko Stocking Co.
7. From D. Smith (Secretary of an engineering firm) complaining that a typewriter supplied by your firm was faulty.
8. A reply to Mr. Smith.
9. Acknowledging a letter of complaint and promising investigation.
10. Complaining to the railway company that goods sent by rail have been damaged on the journey.
11. A reply from the railway company.

21
The Warehouse and the Buyer

**warehouseman   ground floor   basement   lift   transport
gangway storekeeper foreman trolley truck glass partition
commitments   purchases book   stocktaking   cipher
due-card cross-reference supply demand**

After working for about three months in the Sales Department, Olaf is transferred to the warehouse. Here an entirely different world surrounds him. Now he sees at last the goods about which he has read so much in the inquiries, the offers, the orders—and in the complaints.

The warehouse is a very big place; it covers almost the whole ground floor and the greater part of the basement. A goods-lift connects the two floors and allows easy transport up- and downstairs. On long rows of shelves which are divided by gangways lie hundreds of pieces of goods of every description, and it seems to Olaf almost impossible to keep the place in order or to find what one wants. But he soon sees how it is done. The merchandise is stored according to articles, qualities, and categories, and within these, in strict numerical order. At the head of every shelf is a board showing exactly what articles are stored on this shelf. Storekeepers and warehousemen under the supervision of a foreman are responsible for keeping the place and the goods clean and in order. For the transport of the pieces of cloth, which are sometimes very heavy, they use trolleys or trucks on rubber wheels.

Divided from the warehouse by a glass partition is the office of Mr. Keen, the firm's Buyer. He is responsible for all purchases, and it is a very heavy responsibility indeed, for on his experience and skill depends to a very large extent the success of the business. For his job a thorough knowledge of markets is absolutely essential and he must know all the many sources of supply. In deciding his policy he has to rely to a considerable degree on the information which he gets from the Sales Manager, with whom he works in very close co-operation. Whenever they meet they discuss the general position of the trade, the articles which are in special demand, the trend and the changes of fashion, and useful hints which often come from the representatives. But the final decision rests with the Buyer and he must not be afraid of introducing novelties which make his collection attractive, individual and interesting.

One of his main duties is the careful watching of the stocks. He must not allow them to go beyond the limits which are given him by the directors and which are based on the figures which are worked out by the Statistical Department.[1] On the other hand he must not let the stocks fall below a certain level, because that would make the prompt execution of orders difficult. Years of long experience have taught Mr. Keen to strike a happy medium between the two extremes, which depend on current supply and demand.

For the orders he gives, he uses a special order book with three carbon copies. The original is handed or sent to the supplier, one copy goes to the Filing Department, one to the purchases control in the Statistical Department and one is kept in his book. When the goods have been received, that order-copy is removed and from the copies still in his book he can at any moment work out the total number of outstanding orders and analyse them according to the months when they are due. This enables him and the management to estimate the firm's commitments month by month with reasonable accuracy. All orders for later delivery are entered on manufacturers' due-cards. From these he can see which orders are overdue and so can take the necessary action. If stocks grow quicker than sales, his limits will be reduced and he has to adjust his policy

---

[1] For the work of the Statistical Department see page 188ff.

accordingly. Mr. Keen knows most of the suppliers from long personal acquaintance and he spends a good part of the year travelling to the various manufacturing centres always on the lookout for new lines or special bargains.

When a supplier despatches an order to his customer he will sometimes send him an Advice Note, though many firms today prefer to post the invoice on the day of despatch. This invoice serves at the same time as an Advice Note. When the goods arrive at the warehouse, Mr. Keen is informed and he examines every piece very carefully. He compares it with the original pattern and makes sure that quality, weight, colour and finish are correct and satisfactory. After he has passed them 'O.K.' they are marked 'received' in the Purchases Book (see page 163), crossed out in his order book, entered on the manufacturers' due-card (see page 140) and finally taken into stock.

Every piece is marked with a label (or ticket) which gives the piece number, quality, shade and length. At the same time the storekeeper writes out a new card in the stock control index

		NAME	ORDER NUMBER	
PIECE NO.	96/493	Hamilton	1643	10
QUALITY	9009	Brown & Carter	1124	15
SHADE	3	Jackman	1861	10
YARDS	55			
	45			
	30			
	20			

Stock control card

which gives exactly the same details as shown on the label. Every alteration in length is marked on the label whilst the index card shows to whom the various lengths have been sent. If the total amount of these is deducted from the original length of the piece, the index card should show the same measure as the label. At least once a year, at stocktaking, these figures are compared and, if they do not agree, the matter is investigated and adjusted.

Mr. Austin and Mr. Keen have worked out a system by which the piece number shows at once old and slow-moving stocks. The first two figures of the piece number show the year and the month in which the piece has been received; so, for example, the number 36/493 tells them that this is the 493rd piece which was taken into stock in June (the 6th month) 1973. As he goes through the stocks or through the stock lists which are made out at stock-taking, the old numbers will show up at a glance, and Mr Austin is always most anxious to clear them either by reducing the price or by drawing the particular attention of his representatives to these goods.

Olaf notices that at the top and the bottom of the ticket are some letters which do not mean anything to him. In reply to his question he is told that they are 'ciphers' indicating the cost-price and the sales-price to those who know the key. Mr. Keen gives him the secret of Weavewell's cipher word;[1] it is
DUPLICATORS

The letters	D	U	P	L	I	C	A	T	O	R	S
stand for	1	2	3	4	5	6	7	8	9	0	Repeat

the letters D/PS therefore mean £1.33

In a previous chapter we saw how the incoming orders are first examined by the Sales Manager and then passed on to the warehouse for execution. Olaf is, of course, interested to see

[1] Or Code.

how they are dealt with and to watch them on their way through the warehouse.

In the case of orders which are for immediate delivery and can be supplied from stock the procedure is quite simple. A warehouseman (sometimes called a collector) looks out the pieces, the storekeeper cuts off the required lengths, puts on a label which gives the same piece number, quality and shade as the piece label, but only the actual measure of the 'cut-length'. This is then passed with the order to the Invoice Department.

When goods are ordered which are in stock but are not required by the customer until a later date, an order clerk copies the details on to order cards (a separate one for each customer). The goods are reserved for the customer and just before the date when the customer wants the goods the cards are handed to the storekeeper who then arranges for the goods to be invoiced and despatched.

The same order cards are used for 'advance orders', that means orders which are received before the goods are in stock. Weavewell's representatives send such orders in almost every day. But in addition to entering them on the customers' order cards they have to be entered on to the manufacturers' due-cards as well. These due-cards therefore show not only what has been ordered from the manufacturers but at the same time the orders which have been booked for these articles. When the goods come in, the pieces are sent to the various customers accordingly. As the due-cards and the order cards are cross-referenced they show clearly, at any time, how the orders stand and when they are ready for despatch. At the same time the due-cards give the buyer most valuable information as to how the various articles and qualities are selling and show him where he must give repeat orders or what changes and adjustments are required.

Manufacturers' due-card

CROWN MILLS, BRADFORD							
ARTICLE		PRICE	MANUF. REF.		SALES		
9009		£1.69 10.1.73	2531/A		Quant.	Customer	No.
Ordered		Deliv.	Received		Outst.*	30	Hamilton	1643
						21	Street	1124
15.8.	4	Jan.	25.1.	2	2	45/50 2 pcs	Sterling Norman	1861 2261
			3.2.	2	—	16	Wilford	4296
21.9.	8	Feb.			8	35	Nuttall	3318
			22.2.	3	5	24	Jackman	1943
10.1.	4	Apr.	4.3.	3	6	40/45	Wallace	1266
8.4.	6	June	21.4.	4	8			

* Outst. = outstanding = not yet delivered.

Mr. Austin has to go through the order cards three times a month to make sure that all orders are despatched in time. It struck Olaf that this job could be much simplified by using tabs similar to those used in the Filing Department, which would show at a glance which cards require action at a particular date. He mentioned it to Mr. Austin who thought the idea was excellent and he asked Olaf to introduce the system. Within a very short time Olaf completed this scheme, and every order card is now marked with a tab showing the exact time when it has to be dealt with. An 'alarm tab' shows orders which are overdue but not yet ready or complete, and this enables Mr. Austin to take the matter up with the Buyer who in turn puts pressure on the supplier to obtain immediate delivery.

Weavewell Woollen Co. Ltd.
Victoria Street,
London, EC4X ISH

JK/DM 18th February, 19—.

Messrs. Blythe & Co. Ltd.,
3, Carter Lane,
Keighley, Yorks.
BD7 6TY

Dear Sirs,

Our Order No. 4230

On 5th September, 19—, we ordered 40 pieces Melton[1] K for delivery Jan./Feb. You have so far delivered only 14 pieces—6 pieces on 25th January and 8 pieces on 14th February; 26 pieces are therefore overdue.

When we placed the order we pointed out that punctual delivery was of special importance in this case because we had given our customers a definite assurance that we could supply at the beginning of March.

Your delay causes us considerable difficulty and we must ask you to do your utmost to despatch the overdue pieces in the very near future.

Please inform us by return of post when we can expect delivery with certainty so that we can advise our customers, who are threatening to cancel their orders.

                Yours faithfully,
                For Weavewell Woollen Co. Ltd.
                JAMES KEEN

---

[1] Type of cloth.

Weavewell Woollen Co. Ltd.
Victoria Street,
London, EC4X 1SH

JK/DM 1st March, 19—.

Messrs. Werner & Walker Ltd.,
The Quadrant,
Leeds, LS1 1FC

Dear Sirs,

<u>Our Order No. 3962</u>

We refer to our Order No. 3962 of 29th September and should be grateful if you could make the following alterations:

Cancel 10 pieces 1462 and increase 1463 from 6 to 10 pieces and 1464 from 12 to 18 pieces.

Please confirm these alterations which will not, we hope, affect the delivery date.

     Yours faithfully,
     For Weavewell Woollen Co. Ltd.
     JAMES KEEN

Weavewell Woollen Co. Ltd.
Victoria Street,
London, EC4X 1SH

JK/DM 22nd January, 19—.

Messrs. Townsend & Crawley Ltd.,
Huddersfield, HD4 5RE

Dear Sirs,

When your Mr. Kershaw was in London last month we mentioned that we intended to place a repeat order for some of your serges[1] and twills.[1]

[1] Types of cloth.

As wool prices at the last sales were easier, we expect a corresponding reduction of your prices and would be interested to hear what quotations you can offer for orders of 50/100 pieces.

                    Yours faithfully,
              For Weavewell Woollen Co. Ltd.

                    JAMES KEEN

Weavewell Woollen Co. Ltd.
Victoria Street,
London, EC4X 1SH

JK/DM   29th January, 19—.
Messrs. Townsend & Crawley Ltd.,
Huddersfield, HD4 5RE

Dear Sirs,

    We thank you for your letter of 25th January giving us your latest quotations for your serges and twills.

    We are, quite frankly, disappointed that you can offer a reduction of only 1p per yard as compared with the order we gave you last October. You probably know that other firms in your area have adjusted their prices much more drastically.

    You know that we have often given your qualities preference, but you will appreciate that we must buy at competitive prices. Unless you can revise your quotation substantially we shall have to place our order elsewhere. As we have to decide quickly, we should be glad to have your reply by return.

                    Yours faithfully,
              For Weavewell Woollen Co. Ltd.

                    JAMES KEEN

Exercises

I WORD STUDY. *Use each of the following:*

transfer, shelf (plural *shelves*), numerical order (use also alphabetical order), supervision (use also *supervise*), purchase, policy (use also *police, politics, polite*), co-operation, trend, hint, novelties (use also *novelty* as an abstract noun), analyse (also *analysis*), management, estimate (noun and verb), overdue (give three other words beginning with *over*—where *over* has the meaning 'excessively', 'more than', e.g. *overcharge*), reduce (give the corresponding noun. What is an opposite of *reduce*?), adjust, lookout (is this the same as *outlook*?), deduct (what is the opposite?), investigate (use also *investigation*), indicate (noun *indication*), glance, previous, procedure (use also *proceed* and note the difference in spelling), book (as a verb).

II *Note, and use the following phrases from this chapter:*

1. goods of every description; 2. in strict numerical order; 3. under the supervision of; 4. responsible for; 5. a heavy responsibility; 6. to a considerable degree; 7. in very close co-operation; 8. the trend of fashion; 9. the final decision rests with; 10. to go beyond the limits; 11. below a certain level; 12. the prompt execution of orders; 13. to strike a happy medium; 14. between the two extremes; 15. the total number of outstanding orders; 16. to estimate the firm's commitments; 17. with reasonable accuracy; 18. take the necessary action; 19. to adjust his policy accordingly; 20. passed to the warehouse for execution; 21. for immediate delivery; 22. supply and demand.

III *Answer the following:*

1. In what part of Weavewell's building is the warehouse? 2. What is the advantage of a goods-lift? 3. Where, and how, is the merchandise stored? 4. Who is responsible for keeping the goods clean and in order? 5. What is used for the transport of very heavy goods? 6. What is the Buyer responsible for? 7. What knowledge is absolutely essential for his job? 8. What helps him in deciding his policy? 9. What points will the Sales Manager discuss with the Buyer? 10. Why must he not let

THE WAREHOUSE AND THE BUYER 145

the stocks fall below a certain level? 11. What does he use for the orders he gives? 12. How can the Buyer estimate the firm's commitments with reasonable accuracy? 13. Where are orders for later delivery entered? 14. What does the Buyer do before goods are finally taken into stock? 15. What details are entered on the label? 16. How can the Sales Manager and the Buyer keep a note of old or slow-moving stock? 17. How will the Sales Manager try to clear this stock? 18. What are 'advance orders'? 19. What do the 'manufacturers' due-cards' show?

IV *Write a short account of:*

(a) the organisation of a warehouse; (b) the work of the Buyer; (c) the use of the Buyer's order book; (d) the value of the 'label'; (e) the working of a 'cipher'; (f) the procedure with orders for immediate delivery from stock; (g) the procedure with 'advance orders'; (h) the law of supply and demand.

22
Invoices

Packing Department sales analysis **pro forma invoice**
specimen carriage paid import licence **currency restrictions**
remittance decimal monetary system Discount Table
calculating machine export invoice sub-total
billing machine parcel value added tax (VAT)

After the goods have been made ready for despatch in the warehouse they are passed with the orders or the order cards to the Invoice Department which is between the warehouse and the Packing and Despatch Department. Olaf visits it regularly to follow the progress of the orders until the goods have actually left the building. A careful check is kept that nothing is sent out before it has been charged to the customer. This is done by means of the invoice, a most important document. An invoice contains all the information which the customer requires and it serves at the same time to keep Weavewell's accounts and records in order. We shall see in a later chapter how the invoices are posted[1] to the customer's account, but they are used for a number of other purposes as well. They form the basis of stock control, sales analysis, statistics and representatives' commission.

Olaf carefully examines some of the invoices that have just been produced. The invoice clerk, Mr. Swift, points out to Olaf that every invoice ought to contain the following details: (1) name and address of the customer; (2) date; (3) order number; (4) description of the goods or quality; (5) piece number; (6) quantity; (7) price; (8) extension; (9) total; (10) method of despatch; (11) terms. Moreover, since April 1973 Weavewell's

[1] Note the two uses of *to post* (1) to mail (a letter, parcel, etc.); (2) to record in an account book.

INVOICES

have had to show (12) Value Added Tax on all their invoices[1], together with their (13) VAT registration number and (14) the exact date of supply (The 'Tax Point').

Here is the invoice for R. L. Street & Co. Ltd., Chester, on which these items are marked, and Olaf studies them and tries to memorise them:

INVOICE

No. 86460

[1] Messrs. R. L. Street & Co. Ltd.,
156, North Street,
Chester, CH2 1GS

[2] 13th December 19—.

Bought of

Weavewell Woollen Co. Ltd.

**Victoria Street,
London, EC4X 1SH**

[13] VAT Registration No. 912 3456 78
[3] Your order No. 1025   [14] Tax Point: 13th December 19—.

[4] Quality	[5] Piece	[6] Length	[7] Price	£
9009	96234	20 yds.	£1.91	[8] 38.20
7642	94948	20 yds.	£1.75	[8] 35.00
8347	99642	20 yds.	£1.89	[8] 37.80
2428	87394	20 yds.	£1.84	[8] 36.80
				£147.80

[1] But certain goods (e.g. food and books) are not taxed at present, and all exports are free of tax.

[12] VAT @ 10% on discounted price* 14.41
(Tax strictly NET)

[9] £162.21

[10] By Passenger Train   [11] Terms: 30 days/2½%
Carriage paid.†
E. & O.E.‡

---

*That is, VAT is calculated on £144.10 (£147.80 less 2½%).
†Carriage Paid means that the sender pays the cost of transport. Carriage Forward means that the cost of transport is paid by the person to whom the goods are sent.
‡E. & O.E. = Errors and omissions excepted.

In many cases additional information is required. On the invoice below for Brown & Carter Ltd., Liverpool, for example, a trade discount (15) has been granted and has to be deducted from the sub-total (9a), a charge for packing is made (16), and the marks of the bales must be given (17).

INVOICE

No. 86469

[1] Messrs. Brown & Carter, Ltd.,
Ushfield House,
Liverpool, L3 3TC

[2] 13th December 19—.

Bought of

Weavewell Woollen Co. Ltd.

**Victoria Street,
London, EC4X 1SH**

[13] VAT Registration No. 912 3456 78
[3] Your Order No. 6143/Export 4022
[14] Tax Point: 13th December 19—.

[4] Quality	[5] Piece No.	[6] Length	[7] Price	£
Gab. 4	96491	55½		
Gab. 4	96494	49		
Gab. 4	96495	52½		
		157 yds.	£1.45	[8]227.65
Gab. 101	93108	46		
Gab. 101	93243	44		
		90 yds.	£1.08	[8]97.20
Gab. 115	84346	53		
Gab. 115	91670	54		
		107 yds.	£0·99	[8]105.93

[9a]£430.78
[15] less 5%   21.54

[9a]£409.24
[16] Packing   3.50

[9a]£412.74
[12] VAT at 10% on discounted price   39.90
(Tax strictly NET)

[9] £452.64

[10] By Goods Train   [11]Terms: 30 days/2½%
Carr. forward
[17] 2 Bales
  B C 101/2
   L

E. & O.E.

CHAPTER 22

The Pro Forma Invoice

Occasionally, though not very often, a special type of invoice is required, called a 'pro forma invoice'. It is similar to the normal invoice in almost every respect but there is one essential difference: the goods shown on it are *not* despatched to the customer but are held until either payment or further instructions have been received. In the home trade the pro forma invoice is generally used in cases where the supplier is not willing to give a certain customer credit and demands payment before delivery (see the specimen below). In the export trade it is frequently the customer who asks for the pro forma invoice, because it gives him complete information of all costs and charges, which he may need in order to apply for an import licence or for the currency in countries where import restrictions or currency restrictions are in force.

PRO FORMA INVOICE

No. 336

Messrs. Johnston & Lucas,
156, City Road,
London, E3R 1LU

16th December 19—.

Bought of

**Weavewell Woollen Co. Ltd.
Victoria Street,
London, EC4X 1SH**

Your Order No.: Tel.

Quality	Piece No.	Length	Price	£	
456/3	82471	46 yds.	76p	34	96

Goods will be despatched on receipt of your remittance.

INVOICES

Calculations   the Discount Tables

OLAF: You know, Mr. Swift, I can't understand how you work out invoices in England with all the complicated weights and measures that you have. I know that your money is now decimal, and that your export business is done with metric measures, but you still use yards[1], feet and inches, and pounds and ounces, in much of your home trade.

MR. SWIFT: I suppose we have had these rather complicated measurements for so long that we don't realise how difficult they can appear to people who are not used to them. And as for the question of working out invoices, machines do all the

'... the machine does the calculations at breath taking speed'

'donkey work' now, thank goodness. If I want to reckon a discount myself, I refer to the Discount Tables, which show at a glance the different percentages of any amount of money. For difficult calculations, I use this—an electric calculating

---

[1] 1 yard = 3 feet = 0.9 metres
   1 foot = 12 inches = 0.3 metres
   1 pound = 16 ounces = 0.45 kilogrammes
   1 ton = 20 hundredweights = 2240 lbs. = 1016 kg.

The usual abbreviations are: oz. (ounce), lb. (pound), cwt. (hundredweight), in. (inch), ft. (foot), yd. (yard).

machine. It looks a little difficult to use at first, but after a little practice you can do addition, subtraction, multiplication and division on it quite easily. The machine does the calculations at breathtaking speed and—what is more—it never makes a mistake.

The preparation of the invoices is now done automatically at Weavewell's. Normally at least four copies of every invoice are produced (although for export invoices there may be several more): the original is sent to the customer, one copy is kept in numerical order (for every invoice has its number) in the Invoice Department, one is passed to the Accounts Department (see page 162ff), one copy is used for the representative's information and the working out of his commission, and the fourth copy, which is narrower than the other three and does not show prices and amounts, serves as instructions for the Packing Department. It is enclosed with the goods and so acts at the same time as an Advice Note for the customer, who can check the parcel or the bale on arrival even if the invoice is not at hand.

and—what is more—it never makes a mistake'

INVOICES

Exercises

I WORD STUDY. *Use the following:*
despatch, progress (as noun and verb), check (compare with *cheque*), document, to post (use with two different meanings), basis, details, extension (note the several uses, e.g. 'an *extension* to the warehouse', 'to work for the *extension* of the business'; in telephoning—'Is that 01-173-7431? Will you give me *extension* 142?' Is the *extension* of the business the same as *the extent* of the business? Explain the difference. Note the special meaning of *extension*, i.e. amount which is part of a total, on page 146), memorise (what is the corresponding noun?), passenger train (goods go quicker by 'passenger train' than by 'goods train'), narrow (what is the opposite?), borne (how does this differ from *born*?), complicated, weight (what is the corresponding verb?), practice (how does this differ from *practise*?), calculate (and *calculation*), subtraction (give the verbs corresponding to *subtraction, addition, multiplication, division*).

II *Use the following phrases from this chapter in sentences of your own:*
1. ready for despatch; 2. a careful check; 3. charged to the customer; 4. posted to the customer's account; 5. they form the basis; 6. additional information; 7. in almost every respect; 8. one essential difference; 9. payment before delivery; 10. all costs and charges; 11. restrictions are in force; 12. on receipt of your remittance; 13. not at hand; 14. with a little practice.

III *Explain briefly:*
1. Carriage paid; 2. Carriage forward; 3. goods train; 4. a calculating machine; 5. Discount Tables.

IV What details ought an invoice to contain?

V What is a pro forma invoice? What is its main use:
(a) in the home trade; (b) in the export trade?

VI Make out an invoice for the following and deduct $2\frac{1}{2}\%$ discount: 3 doz. shirts @ £2·50 each; 3 doz. pairs socks @ 35p each; 45 yds. cloth @ 80p per yd.; 3 doz. ties @ 95p each.

23
Debit and Credit Notes, Delivery Orders and Advice Notes

**Debit Note   overcharge   undercharge   standard qualities
'pending instructions'   docks   bonded warehouse   crate
cubic feet   cross-check   freight   van**

Besides issuing invoices for goods which have been despatched to customers, the Invoice Department has to make out Debit and Credit Notes. These documents are required for adjustments of various kinds. An error in an invoice, an allowance granted for special reasons, returns of goods or packing material are all adjusted either by Debit Note (D/N) or Credit Note (C/N). In order to distinguish between the two and to make mistakes impossible, Credit Notes are always printed in red. Debit and Credit Notes are filed in special files and are kept separate from the invoices. Usually they are posted once a week to the customers' accounts. By going through the files of Debit and Credit Notes at regular intervals the Sales Manager or the Directors can readily check how many mistakes have been made and who has been responsible for them; they can then take the necessary steps to prevent similar errors in future.

Let us look at a few cases where they are used. In a previous chapter we saw that Beach & Sons, Stockport, returned two pieces of Bouclé because of the unsatisfactory colour. This is the C/N which was sent to them with the Sales Manager's letter:

DEBIT AND CREDIT NOTES

CREDIT NOTE (red)

No. 496
15th November, 19—.

Messrs. F. R. Beach & Sons,
Stockport, SK1 7PL
Credited by

Weavewell Woollen Co. Ltd.
Victoria Street,
London, EC4X 1SH

By Return:
Bouclé 93640 $46\frac{1}{4}$
   „   93641 51
           ——
           $97\frac{1}{4}$ @ 87p £84.61

With reference to our letter of today.

The student may remember the error that had crept into the invoice of Brown & Carter Ltd., Liverpool. The Sales Manager had written a most apologetic letter (see pages 130-1) and the following Credit Note was enclosed:

CREDIT NOTE (red)

No. 504
17th December, 19—.

Messrs. Brown & Carter Ltd.,
Ushfield House,
Liverpool, L3 3TC
Credited by

Weavewell Woollen Co. Ltd.
Victoria Street,
London, EC4X 1SH

By Overcharge on our invoice 86469 of 13.12.19—.
 Gab. 4 charged at £1.45 should have been £1.35
 = 157 yds. at 10p £15.70
                                      less 5%   78
                                               ——————
                                               £14.92

If the mistake was an Undercharge a D/N would be used like the following:

DEBIT NOTE

No. 1463
10th January, 19—.

Messrs. Murphy & Hale Ltd.,
16, Barnstaple Road,
Exeter, EX3 6NH
Debit to

Weavewell Woollen Co. Ltd.
Victoria Street,
London, EC4X 1SH

To Undercharge on our invoice No. 96471
 Elasto 97431 charged 46¼ yds.
 should have been   56¼ yds.
 = 10 yds. at £1.89 . . . . . . £18.90
With apologies.

Delivery Orders and Advice Notes

In addition to their stock held in London, Weavewell's have a big warehouse in Bradford, the Weavewell Woollen Co. (Yorkshire) Ltd., where they keep many pieces of their standard cloth. Whenever possible, orders are despatched from there direct to

DEBIT AND CREDIT NOTES

the customer. This saves a considerable amount of time, work and expense. All the mills in the Bradford area deliver regularly to the warehouse and the pieces are held at the disposal of the London house 'pending instructions'. For these instructions Delivery Orders (D/O) are used. When, for example, the order from Murphy & Hale Ltd., Exeter, for 7 pieces of 'Elasto' is received (see pages 105-7) a Delivery Order is sent to Bradford which reads as follows:

DELIVERY ORDER

No. 2240 W/B
15th December, 19—.

Weavewell Woollen Co. Ltd.
Victoria Street,
London, EC4X 1SH

Weavewell Woollen Co. (Yorkshire) Ltd.,
Percival Buildings, Bradford, BD1 0DR
  Please deliver to:
    Messrs. Murphy & Hale Ltd.,
      16, Barnstaple Road, Exeter, EX3 6NH
Order No. 1649

1 piece Elasto	January		
1 ,, ,,	February		
2 ,, ,,	March	By Rail.
2 ,, ,,	April	Marks: W Y
1 ,, ,,	May	9

  1 Advice Note to be encl.
  2 ,,   ,, to us.

On receipt of this D/O the foreman of the Bradford warehouse makes the necessary entries in his stock control and reserves the pieces for delivery at the required time. When the first piece is due it is sent to Exeter and an Advice Note (A/N), with three copies, is typed; the original is packed with the goods, one copy is kept on the Bradford file, and two copies are posted to London:

ADVICE NOTE

No. 4632 W/B

Weavewell Woollen Co. Ltd.
Percival Buildings,
Bradford, BD1 0DR

6th January, 19—.

Despatched to:
    Messrs. Murphy & Hale Ltd.,
        16, Barnstaple Road, Exeter, EX3 6NH.
1 piece Elasto No. 97431, $56\frac{1}{4}$ yds.   Order No. 1649
  Rest to follow Feb./May.
  By Rail
  Marks: W Y
        9

On the basis of this Advice Note the London house makes out the invoice for the customer. For clarity, details of value added tax (see page 147) have been omitted from this example.

INVOICE

Messrs. Murphy & Hale Ltd.,   96471
16, Barnstaple Road,
Exeter, EX3 6NH   7th January, 19—.
Bought of

Weavewell Woollen Co. Ltd.
Victoria Street,
London, EC4X 1SH

DEBIT AND CREDIT NOTES

Your Order No. 1649

Quality	Piece No.	Length	Price	£	p
Elasto	97431	46¼	£1.89	87	31
By Rail					
1 Bale					
W Y	direct from our Bradford Warehouse				
9			Terms: 30 days 2½%		

A copy of this invoice is returned with the copy of the Advice Note to Bradford and so there is no risk of overlooking the charge for goods supplied direct. If there is any mistake it will be found when the two documents are compared in Bradford. This cross-check is essential because experience has shown that errors occur much more frequently where the actual goods cannot be compared with the Packing Note. A careful student will probably have noticed that the Advice Note and the invoice do not agree (the correction will be found on page 156).

The pieces for delivery in February, March, April and May will be despatched by Bradford at the dates mentioned and every time this is done an Advice Note will be sent to London for the purpose of charging the customer.

Of course, Delivery Orders and Advice Notes are not used only between Weavewell's and their Bradford warehouse but in all cases where instructions are given to transfer goods from one place to another, for example, from docks to warehouse or from bonded[1] warehouse to a customer.

We mentioned on page 152 that the last copy of the invoice-set serves as packing instructions and as Advice Note. It is handed to the Packing and Despatch Department where it is carefully checked with the goods. Every item is compared and

---

[1] *A bonded warehouse* is one under the control of the Customs authorities although it is owned by a private firm. Goods (e.g. those for re-export or those for which there is at present no buyer) can be kept here without payment of duty. (See *A Commercial Course for Foreign Students*, Vols. I and II.)

marked off, and when all is found correct the goods are packed and the Advice Note put on top. According to the quantity they are either packed in parcels with strong paper and string, or in bales wrapped in paper and sewn in jute.[1] For bigger quantities, and especially for export, wooden cases and crates are used. They are lined with waterproof material to prevent damage by dampness and very often are made to the exact measurements which are required, because freight is calculated on cubic feet or metres, and skilful packing may save a lot of money. For that reason this job is often given to firms of export packers who specialise in this work.

Parcels are despatched either by post or by carrier, bales by carrier or rail, and cases and crates by rail or boat. For deliveries in London Weavewell's use their own van.

Exercises

I WORD STUDY. *Use the following:*

issue (noun and verb), adjust (also *adjustment*), error, unsatisfactory (use also *satisfactory, satisfaction, satisfy, dissatisfaction, dissatisfied*), 'pending instructions' (it means 'while we are waiting for your instructions'), due, overlook (is this the same as 'look over'?), docks (be careful with the pronunciation [dɔks]. Don't make it sound like 'dogs' [dɔgz]), string (what is the difference between *string* and *rope*?), sew [sou] (give the principal parts of the verb. How does it differ from *sow* pronounced also [sou], and *sow* pronounced [sau]?), specialise.

II *Note the use of* make *in the phrases:*

to make out Debit Notes;
to make out the invoice.

There are many uses of this verb and these can only be learned by experience. Here are some examples. Try to explain the meaning of each. 1. That firm *made* a lot of *money* last year. 2. He *makes his living* by *making* shoes. 3. Two and two *make* four. 4. The firm have just *made* Mr. Austin *Sales Manager*.

---

[1] Jute = a plant, part of which is used for making sacking and rope.

DEBIT AND CREDIT NOTES

5. You are *making good progress* with your work. 6. The invoice clerk *made a mistake*. 7. We shall *make it our business* to satisfy our customer. 8. If we can't change things we must *make the best* of it. 9. *Make sure* that you have included the Advice Note. 10. The ship is *making for port* as fast as it can. 11. I can't *make out* this customer's handwriting. 12. The old man has *made over* his property to his son. 13. The office boy has just *made the tea*. 14. '*Make hay* while the sun shines' (Proverb). 15. The servant *made the beds* in the hotel. 16. 'As you *make* your bed so you must lie on it' (Proverb). 17. He loves *making jokes*. 18. I am going to *make my will*. 19. You have *made up* that story; it isn't true. 20. The girl put *make-up* on her face (or *made* her face *up*).

III *Answer the following:*

1. Give the abbreviations for Debit Note, Credit Note, Advice Note, Delivery Order. 2. What are Debit Notes and Credit Notes used for? 3. What colour are Credit Notes? Why? 4. When is a Delivery Order used? 5. Explain what the foreman of a warehouse does when he receives a Delivery Order. 6. How many copies of an Advice Note are typed out? What is done with each of them? 7. When is there likely to be a risk of overlooking a charge? What precautions are taken to avoid the risk? 8. What is a 'bonded warehouse'? 9. How are goods packed? 10. How are they despatched?

IV 1. Weavewell's want to send pieces of cloth at five different dates to Messrs. Lloyd & Baker. Make out the Delivery Order.

2. Lloyd & Baker have been overcharged on an invoice by £2·84. Make out the Credit Note.

3. Smith & Thompson have been undercharged by £3·09. Make out the Debit Note.

4. The Bradford factory sends goods for Weavewell's direct to Cook & Blackwell. Make out the Advice Note and on the basis of this make out the invoice from Weavewell's to the customer.

24
Accounts (1)

**Ledger   Purchases Book   Purchases Ledger   Sales Book
Cash Received Book   Cash Paid Book   sales control
enter (entry)   Statistics (statistical)   Loose Leaf Ledger
Sundry Account   Petty Cash Book   adding machine
paying-in slip   to 'cast' accounts**

Early in February Mr. Brown had another chat with Olaf and suggested that he should now move into the Accounts Department. 'You must have a fairly good idea of our organisation by now,' he said, 'and you will find that, in one way or other, all that is done in the various departments is reduced to figures and recorded in the accounts.'

Olaf did not need an introduction to Mr. Smithson, who is the Secretary of the company and is in charge of the Accounts Department, for Olaf's work in the other departments had frequently taken him into 'the Accounts'. Mr. Smithson gave him 'in a nutshell' the lines on which this important department is organised. 'You must imagine, Petersen, that there are two movements that we are recording here, one of goods and one of payments. Goods are bought from our suppliers and come into the house; they are sold to our customers and sent out.' While he

Movement of goods and payments

was speaking he picked up a pencil and illustrated what he meant by a diagram.

'We receive payments from the customer and we make payments to the supplier. That's simple enough, isn't it?'

'Quite simple,' said Olaf.

'Good,' continued Mr. Smithson. 'Now then, let's see how we in the Accounts Department record these movements. Goods which we have bought from suppliers, that is, our purchases, are charged to us on invoices which are entered into the Purchases Book.' Again he got to work with a pencil making another diagram as he talked (page 164).

'From the Purchases Book they are credited to the supplier's account in the Purchases (or Bought) Ledger.'

OLAF: Oh yes, that little diagram makes it easy.

MR. SMITHSON: Good. Let's continue the diagram, then, from Weavewell's to the customer. When we sell the goods we invoice them to our customers; you saw that, of course, in the Invoice Department. A copy of every invoice comes to us. Some firms post these invoices into a special Sales Book. We don't, we file these copies in numerical order and treat that file as our Sales Book. From there they are debited direct to the customer's account in the Sales Ledger. That saves a lot of time—and mistakes. So much for the one movement, goods.

Now let's take the other movement, payments.

Payments which we make to our suppliers are noted in this Cash Paid Book and are debited to the respective accounts. Payments received from our customers are entered into the Cash Received Book and from there are credited to the customers' ledger accounts (see page 166).

I remember, years ago, we had only one Cash Book into which the cash received was entered on the debit side and the cash paid was entered on the credit side, but we found it much more convenient to split it up into two books, because now one clerk can enter the payments that have come in, while another

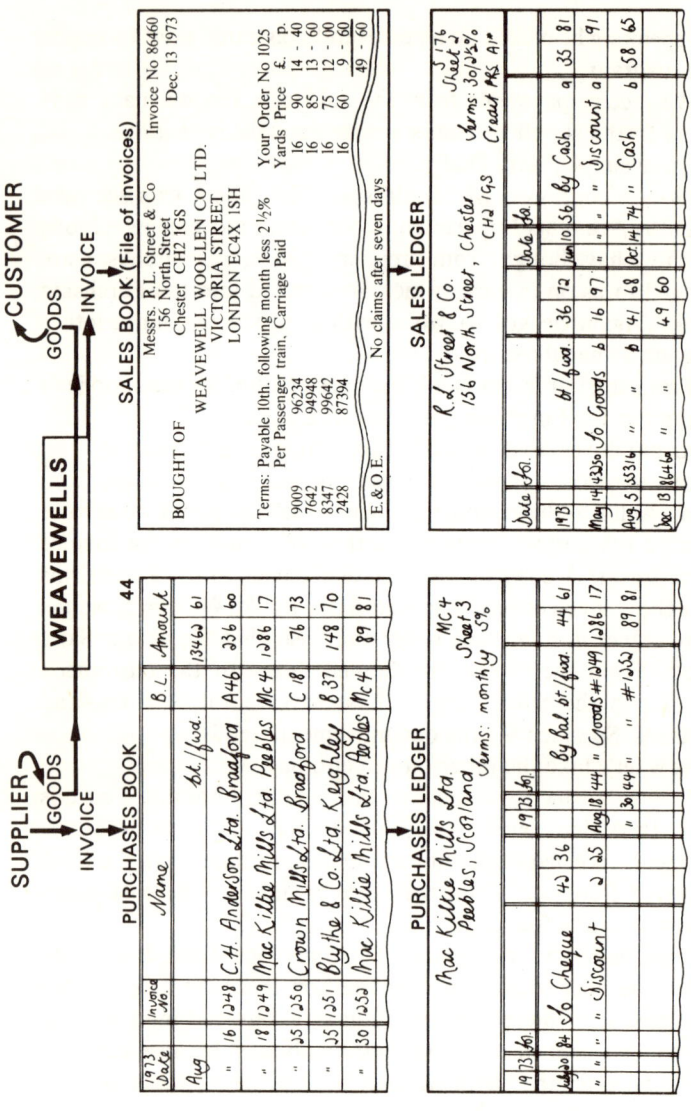

"Let's see how we in the Accounts Department record these movements"

ACCOUNTS (1)

can work on the Cash Paid Book for payments going out. The control of the Cash Books is almost automatic: all payments are made by cheque and the cash received is paid into the bank daily. At the end of the month we get the bank's statement and, obviously, everything that has been posted into our Cash Books must sooner or later appear in these statements. Well, all that will become much clearer to you when you start posting the books yourself.

With these words he introduces Olaf to one of the ledger clerks and after a few explanations Olaf is given the job of posting the Sales Book to the Ledger. He finds that, in fact, things are a little more complicated than Mr. Smithson's explanation had suggested: there are separate Sales Books and Ledgers for town customers, country sales and exports, and the Cash Received Book has separate columns for these three categories. Olaf realises later that this division is of great assistance for the sales control and for the statistical information which the firm requires (see pages 188-90).

For several weeks Olaf works under the supervision and instruction of Mr. Smithson; he enters purchases invoices, posts the sales, and writes up the Cash Books. He learns how to insert new accounts in strict alphabetical order into the loose leaf Ledgers, how to open accounts, and how to mark the terms and the credit limit. He finds it quite fascinating to see how from these various entries an intricate system of accounts is built up, which shows at a glance the exact position of every customer and supplier.

Every firm with whom Weavewell's have regular dealings has its own account in the Bought (Purchases) Ledger or in one of the various Sales Ledgers. There are, of course, some firms who buy only occasionally and for whom no separate account is necessary. For these firms a 'Sundry Account' is kept under every letter and an occasional sale to Armstrong, for example, is posted to 'A' Sundries, one to Burton is posted to 'B' Sundries, and so on.

SUPPLIER PAYMENTS → **WEAVEWELLS** ← **CUSTOMER PAYMENTS**

CASH PAID BOOK 96

1973 Date	Cheque Number	Name	Fol.	bt/fwd Discount	Amount	Recpt No.
Sept 20	04432	C H Anderson Bradford	A 46	226 71	4368 85	—
" 20	" 33	MacKillie Mills Ltd	Mc 4	5 82	330 70	763
" 27	" 34	B C Lawson & Keighley	L 23	64 38*	1221 79	769
" 27	" 35	C H Walter Ltd	W 6	13 26	78 15	766
					160 59	768

PURCHASERS LEDGER

Mac Killie Mills Ltd. Mc 4
Peebles, Scotland   Sheet 3
Terms: monthly 5%.

1973	Fol.				1973	Fol.			
July 30	84	To Cheque	42 36		July 30		By Bal. bt/fwd	44 61	
" "	"	" Discount	2 25		Aug 18	44	" Goods + # 1249	1286 17	
Sept 30	96	" Cheque	1221 79	Aug 30	44	" " # 1052	89 81	
" "	"	" Discount	64 38						

CASH RECEIVED BOOK 123

Date	Name	Fol.	bt/fwd Discount	Town	County	Export	Amount	Bank
			bank Leicester					3461 92
May 5	S C Hamilton Co	H 71	8 84 40		16 83		16 83	
July 11	R L Street Co	ST 4			34 30		34 30	
Sept 2	Hilto Ltd London		5 14 1 24		48 36		48 36	
Sept 13	J H Wynman	38	1 44 1 93	74 71			74 71	
Oct 4	Jas Guerra Madras	W 9		14 84			14 84	
Dec 1	A Numba Barcelona	R 17	3 12			22 52	22 52	
Dec 16			6 7			46 90	46 90	
Dec 21			3 32		129 40		129 40	470 25

SALES LEDGER

R L Street and Co.   Sheet 376
156 North Street, Chester.   Terms: 30/15%
CH.4/G5   Credit PRS A1

Date	Fol.				Date	Fol.			
		bt/fwd	36 72		Jan 10	56	By Cash a	35 81	
May 14	4320	To Goods b	16 91		" "	"	" Discount	91	
Aug 5	5534	" " b	41 68		Oct 14	74	" Cash b	58 65	
Dec 13	8446	" " c	49 60		Jan 1973 24	103	" Cash c	48 36	
					" "	"	" Discount c	1 24	

Recording the movement of payments

ACCOUNTS (I)

The Purchases Book, the Sales Books, the Cash Books, the Bought Ledger and the various Sales Ledgers form together what is known as a 'set of books'. There are a number of other smaller books; one of them is the 'Petty Cash Book' into which are entered small expenses like fares, tips, etc.

All the books have, of course, to be added up and Olaf is much relieved to find that the department has adding machines for this purpose which make the job easy and almost pleasant. Accounts are cast,[1] the total carried forward (c/fd) at the bottom and brought forward (b/fd) at the top of the new page. The sum of the cash received on each day must correspond with the total of the paying-in slip that goes to the bank. The Sales Books are added up and compared with the figures supplied by the Invoice Department. Yes, there is a keen demand for the machines all day long. There is, however, one job which Olaf doesn't like. Some customers still want receipts for their

---

Weavewell Woollen Co. Ltd. No. B.8334

VICTORIA STREET LONDON EC4X 1SH

Received from........Dean and Stowe........

the sum of........Ninety four........Pounds

Twenty five........pence

With Thanks WEAVEWELL WOOLLEN CO. LTD.

£ 94.25

Date 23rd February 19—.

J. Smithson
Secretary

Receipt form

[1] *cast* = reckoned; added up.

payments though these are not really necessary if payment is by cheque. Weavewell's use special receipt forms which are filled in with the date, the customer's name and the amount and which are signed by the secretary or one of the clerks.

Exercises

I WORD STUDY. *Use the following:*

enter (also *entry*) as used in this chapter, introduce (use also *introduction*. Note the difference in pronunciation [intrə'djuːs], [intrə'dʌkʃn]. Compare *reduce, reduction*), diagram, respective (this is rather a difficult word to use. Here are some examples:
> I want you to mark these three samples with their *respective* prices.
> The four books were sent to their *respective* owners.
> The three samples of cloth were marked £1.73, £1.85 and £1.96 *respectively*.

Don't confuse it with *respect, respectable, respectably*), split, automatic, obvious (also *obviously*), to *post* books (note the different use of *post* in 'to *post* a letter'), supervision [sjuːpə'viʒn] (also *supervise* ['sjuːpəvaiz]; note the difference in pronunciation), insert, fascinate (also *fascinating, fascination*), intricate ['intrikit], affix (noun ['æfiks] verb [ə'fiks]), condense (what is *condensed* milk?).

II In this chapter you had the following words or phrases: a *set* of books; *tips*; a paying-in *slip*. Here are examples of different uses of these words. Explain each and make other examples:

set

He *set* fire to the building.
She *set* the birds free.
The maid *set the table*.
I have never *set foot* in that office.
Mr. Smithson *set an example* of hard work.
The traveller *set off* for Manchester with the latest samples.
Olaf *set to work* on the Sales Book.

ACCOUNTS (1)

The loss of the export market in Brazil was a bad *set-back* to our business.

The customer ordered three *sets* of Shakespeare's plays and four *sets* of Scott's novels.

tip

Olaf gave a *tip* to the taxi-driver. He also *tipped* the porter 10p.

Take my *tip* and buy these goods now—the price is going to rise.

The *tips* of his fingers were blue with cold.

Mr. Smithson has all the details of the office work at his *finger-tips*.

slip

Write the price on this *slip* of paper.

The horse *slipped* on the frozen road. The ice had made the stones very *slippery*.

Olaf *slipped out* of the room quietly.

You have *made a slip* in adding up this account.

I shouldn't have said that; it was a *slip of the tongue*.

I meant to write to Armstrong & Co. today, and it quite *slipped my memory*.

I tried to catch the office boy before he went home but he *gave me the slip*.

III What would you enter into (a) the Purchases Book; (b) the Bought Ledger; (c) the Sales Book; (d) the Cash Received Book; (e) the Sales Ledger; (f) a paying-in slip; (g) a Sundries Account; (h) the Petty Cash Book?

(1) Describe (a) how purchases are recorded; (b) how payments are recorded in the Accounts Department.
(2) Explain the advantage of having separate 'Cash Paid' and 'Cash Received' books.
(3) How can you check the accuracy of the Cash Books?
(4) What is a 'set of books'?

25
Accounts (2)

To render statements   item   approved accounts
financial standing   overdue   copy invoice   Debt Collection Letter
Cash with Order (C.W.O.)   Cash on Delivery (C.O.D.)
trade reference   bank reference   credit status   trademark
deal   stamped addressed envelope   liabilities   sanction
Status Inquiry Agency (Mercantile Agency)   writ
standard form

At the end of the month the statements have to be rendered. These statements contain in a condensed form all the entries that have been made on the customers' accounts. This enables the customer to check his books with the statement and to see whether both agree. At the bottom the statement shows the balance of the account and the discount, if any. Most of Weavewell's statements are marked with a rubber stamp:

> Subject to $2\frac{1}{2}$% Discount
> if settled within 30 days

A number of accounts, especially in export, are rendered quarterly; but the majority, totalling several hundred, are sent out at the end of each month. This used to be a considerable job, occupying the whole department for several days. But now Weavewell's have introduced an automatic system which posts the ledgers, prepares the statements, prints the receipt-slips and even provides a control sheet 'in one go'.

The main purpose of the statement is, of course, to act as a request for payment. When the customer receives it, he checks it with his books, and if he agrees he 'passes it for payment'. A cheque for the balance shown is made out and returned to

Weavewell's with their statement; no letter is necessary in this case. Sometimes, however, the customer may not be able to find an invoice in his account which is shown on the statement. He then marks that item on the statement: 'No trace, copy please', and sends it back, and Weavewell's send him a 'Copy Invoice' by return of post.

Within a few days after the statements have been rendered, the number of incoming payments swells considerably and after a fortnight a very great number of customers have settled their balances. Most of them pay within 30 days in order to take advantage of the discount, others pay within 60 days net. The way in which a firm settles its accounts is in itself the best indication of its financial standing. A glance at the ledger sheet shows at once the quality of the customer, and this is as important for him as for his supplier. Naturally, a firm that has proved its reliability will receive preferential treatment and will sometimes obtain special concessions. But though Weavewell's are very careful to give credit to 'approved accounts' only, that is to firms where they are satisfied about the financial standing of the customer, there are always a number of accounts left which are overdue. In those cases the balance of the previous statement is shown on the new statement: 'To balance of account rendered' which in itself is a gentle reminder. Very often Mr. Smithson, who goes through all the statements before they are sent out, writes on it a remark such as: 'Please' or 'Please remit and oblige', or, a little stronger, 'Overdue, payment by return will oblige.' Strangely enough these little notes very often do the trick, but if they do not, special application or Debt Collection Letters are sent out at intervals of a week. The first one is short but polite:

CHAPTER 25

First application

Weavewell Woollen Co. Ltd.
Victoria Street,
London, EC4X 1SH

Dear Sirs,

We would remind you that the balance of our September statement amounting to £56.84 is now overdue. Please give this matter your attention and let us have a cheque in settlement at an early date.

                        Yours faithfully,
                 p.p. Weavewell Woollen Co. Ltd.
                     J. SMITHSON
                     Secretary

---

or

Weavewell Woollen Co. Ltd.
Victoria Street,
London, EC4X 1SH

Dear Sirs,

We refer to our September statement showing a balance of £56.84. As this amount is now overdue we shall be grateful to receive your remittance by return.

                        Yours faithfully,
                 p.p. Weavewell Woollen Co. Ltd.
                       J. SMITHSON
                     Secretary

If that does not work, a second letter is sent off which is in somewhat more definite terms:

Second application

Weavewell Woollen Co. Ltd.
**Victoria Street,
London, EC4X 1SH**

Dear Sirs,

With reference to our letter of 16th January asking for payment of the overdue balance of £56.84 we regret that we have not yet received your remittance. We are unable to keep this account open any longer and must request you to let us have your cheque without further delay.

                Yours faithfully,
                p.p. Weavewell Woollen Co. Ltd.

                J. SMITHSON
                Secretary

---

or

Weavewell Woollen Co. Ltd.
**Victoria Street,
London, EC4X 1SH**

Dear Sirs,

We enclose our statement to 31st December, 19—, from which you will see that a balance of £124.66 is due to us. We would point out that the earlier part of the statement is long overdue, some of the items dating back to August and September. We trust that you will give this matter your immediate attention and that we shall receive your cheque within the next few days.

>Yours faithfully,
>p.p. Weavewell Woollen Co. Ltd.
>*J. SMITHSON*
>Secretary

Encl.

In the few cases where even this second application does not have the desired effect, more energetic steps must be taken. The customer is given a last warning:

Third application

Weavewell Woollen Co. Ltd.
Victoria Street,
London, EC4X 1SH

Dear Sirs,

We regret that our repeated applications for a settlement of the overdue balance of our account have been ignored by you. We must inform you that unless your payment is received within 7 days we shall instruct our solicitors to take the necessary steps.

>Yours faithfully,
>p.p. Weavewell Woollen Co. Ltd.
>*J. SMITHSON*
>Secretary

ACCOUNTS (2)

or

Weavewell Woollen Co. Ltd.
Victoria Street,
London, EC4X 1SH

Dear Sirs,

As you have not replied to our various requests for payment of the long overdue items of our account we shall be compelled to take legal proceedings if your cheque does not reach us within 7 days.

       Yours faithfully,
    p.p. Weavewell Woollen Co. Ltd.

      J. SMITHSON
      Secretary

Fortunately, such letters are exceptional as Weavewell's are very careful to grant credit only to firms of good standing and reputation. In doubtful cases the Sales Manager demands Cash with Order (C.W.O.) or supplies only against Cash on Delivery (C.O.D.). Sometimes a pro forma invoice is sent to the customer and the goods are sent out only after payment has been received. A customer of good reputation but one with whom the firm has not had previous dealings will, as a rule, supply trade or bank references with his first order so that inquiries into his credit status can be made. These status inquiries are made by the Accounts Department, generally on instructions from the Sales Manager. Olaf remembers the case of John Sterling & Co., Norwich, which happened just after he had started in the Sales Department (see pages 79 and 110). He turns up the file and finds the following letters:

CHAPTER 25

'. . . we enclose a stamped, addressed envelope for your reply'

Status inquiries

Weavewell Woollen Co. Ltd.
Victoria Street,
London, EC4X ISH

JS/EB
Messrs. Simpson & West,
Bradford, BD1 1PM
12th December, 19—.

Dear Sirs,

We have been referred to you by Messrs. John Sterling & Co., Market Place, Norwich, who want to open an account with us.

We should be obliged if you would let us know whether in your opinion a credit of £200 can be safely granted. Any other information you may be able to give will be welcome and will, of course, be treated in strictest confidence.

ACCOUNTS (2)

Thanking you in anticipation, we enclose a stamped, addressed envelope for your reply,

                      Yours faithfully,
                  p.p. Weavewell Woollen Co. Ltd.
                    J. SMITHSON
                    Secretary

Encl.

Weavewell Woollen Co. Ltd.
Victoria Street,
London, EC4X 1SH

JS/EB   12th December, 19—.
Messrs. Slater & Steel Ltd.,
Fore Street,
London, EC2J 9OJ

Dear Sirs,

    We have received an order amounting to about £200 from Messrs. John Sterling & Co., Norwich, who have given us your name as a reference.

May we ask you to inform us whether you have done business with the above named firm for any length of time and whether you think that their integrity and reputation justify a credit of £200.

We thank you in anticipation and shall be pleased to return the courtesy if occasion arises. A stamped, addressed envelope is enclosed for your reply.

                      Yours faithfully,
                  p.p. Weavewell Woollen Co. Ltd.
                    J. SMITHSON
                    Secretary

Encl.

Replies to status inquiries

Simpson & West
The Square,
Bradford, BD1 1PM

14th December, 19—.

The Secretary,
Weavewell Woollen Co. Ltd.,
Victoria Street,
London, EC4X 1SH

Dear Sir,

In reply to your letter of yesterday we write to inform you that we have known Messrs. Sterling & Co., Norwich, for many years. They have built up an excellent business and are today one of the leading firms in Norwich. Both partners are working in the business, they know their job and are experienced in the trade. Our turnover with them has been growing steadily year by year and is now quite considerable. We have allowed them credits far in excess of the sum you mention.

We give this information without responsibility.

Yours faithfully,
For Simpson & West

A. THOMAS

Secretary

Private and Confidential

Slater & Steel Ltd.
**14, Fore Street,
London, EC2J 9OJ**

14th December, 19—.

The Secretary,
Weavewell Woollen Co. Ltd.,
Victoria Street,
London, EC4X 1SH

Private and Confidential

Dear Sir,

We give you below the information for which you asked in your letter of 12th December.

The firm whose name appears on the attached slip carries on a substantial business; the owners are known to us as reliable and trustworthy men and liabilities have been met regularly and punctually. We have no hesitation in recommending a credit of £200.

This information is given to the best of our knowledge and belief. We cannot, however, accept any responsibility, and trust that you will treat it in strict confidence.

Yours faithfully,
p.p. Slater & Steel Ltd.

J. HART

Accountant

Encl. Slip

On the basis of these very favourable references Mr. Smithson decides to open an account and to grant credit up to £300. This credit limit is marked at the top of the ledger-sheet and any credit in excess of this amount must first be 'sanctioned' by the Secretary or the Sales Manager.

When a customer, in addition to the trade references, gives his bank as a reference as well, this cannot be taken up direct; the bank would write back saying that it is against the custom of banks to give information in reply to private inquiries. In such a case Weavewell's have to write to their own bank and ask them to make the necessary investigations. Here is an example:

Weavewell Woollen Co. Ltd.
Victoria Street,
London, EC4X 1SH

JS/EB   3rd February, 19—.

The Manager,
London & Wessex Bank Ltd.,
Queen Street, EC4D 1ON

Dear Sir,

We have today received an order for £275 from Messrs. Goodwin & Colt Ltd., 43 Great Duke Street, Edinburgh, who have given their bank, the Empire Bank, Fore Street, Edinburgh, as a reference.

We should be obliged if you would make inquiries on our behalf as to whether the reputation and the financial standing of the firm justify a credit of the above amount.

Thanking you in anticipation,

        We are,

                Yours faithfully,
              p.p. Weavewell Woollen Co. Ltd.
              J. SMITHSON
              Secretary

As a rule the information supplied by banks is rather brief and far less personal than that obtained through the trade:

London & Wessex Bank Ltd.
Queen Street,
London, EC4D 1ON

8th February, 19—.

Dear Sir,

G. & C. Ltd., Edinburgh

The above firm has been trading since 1921. Liabilities have been met regularly. The directors are described as efficient and reliable.

A credit of £275 is considered sound.

Without responsibility.

Yours faithfully,
For London & Wessex Bank Ltd.
R. EDGELEY
Manager

The Secretary,
Weavewell Woollen Co. Ltd.,
Victoria Street,
London, EC4X 1SH

About a fortnight after Olaf had entered the Accounts Department, a representative sent a fairly big order from a new customer and, as the representative's report sounded a little doubtful, Mr. Smithson asked Olaf not only to take up the two trade references which had been supplied with the order, but also to make a status inquiry through an independent Mercantile Agency (or 'Status Inquiry Agency'). The trade references looked quite good; both firms had done business with this customer for some time and payments had been made regularly, though in both cases the amounts in question had been fairly small. Olaf was most surprised, therefore, when a few days later this reply came in from the agency:

Inquiries Unlimited
4, Bishopsgate,
London, EC2R 9EV

15th February, 19—.

The Secretary,
Weavewell Woollen Co. Ltd.,
Victoria Street,
London, EC4X 1SH

Dear Sir,

<u>*Your Inquiry 79, OP/EB*</u>

The firm whose name is shown on the enclosed slip was started in 1970 with a capital of £500. The business does not seem to have developed satisfactorily.

It appears that the capital is insufficient for the large stock carried and that the firm finds it difficult to obtain credit. A writ[1] was issued in September last but was later withdrawn. We would mention that we have had several inquiries lately. Our advice is to supply on a cash basis only.

This information is strictly private and confidential and is given without responsibility on the part of the company.

Yours faithfully,
Inquiries Unlimited

F. BLYTHE

Director

Encl. 1 Slip

Olaf pointed out this contradiction to Mr. Smithson, but he smiled and said: 'I was expecting something like that; that's why

---

[1] A legal document issued by a court ordering a person to do something (e.g. pay his debts) or cease doing something (e.g. imitating another firm's trademark).

ACCOUNTS (2)

I asked you to take it up with our agency. You see, firms like this one often owe money all over the place, but they always keep their accounts with a few firms in order and they use these firms as references. Independent agencies, however, have a vast store of information in their records. They receive inquiries from many sides and have experienced agents in all important centres, and they soon find out whether a firm is sound or not. Yes, you can't watch your accounts too carefully.'

It goes without saying that the order from that firm is marked 'Cash in Advance'. A pro forma invoice is sent to them with a request for payment but when, in spite of two reminders, no reply is received, the order is 'scrapped'.

There is, of course, a certain amount of correspondence in the Accounts Department, though every effort is made to reduce it to the minimum. Wherever possible, printed standard forms are used for all routine transactions. But in spite of all precautions mistakes happen, and they have to be adjusted by individual letters. There is, for example, the case of a customer who had asked for a Copy Invoice because he could not trace an item which appeared on the statement. When the original invoice was looked up it was found that an error had been made and the following letter was written:

Weavewell Woollen Co. Ltd.
Victoria Street,
London, EC4X 1SH

JS/EB 20th February, 19—.

Messrs. Mason & Andrews, Ltd.,
14, Church Road,
Woking, GU8 8CG

Dear Sirs,

We very much regret that, owing to a clerical mistake, invoice No. 43678 was posted to your account in error and consequently shown in our statement. We have now transferred this item to the correct account and ask you to accept our apologies for this mistake and the trouble it has caused you.

Please find enclosed our corrected statement, which we trust you will find in order.

>Yours faithfully,
>p.p. Weavewell Woollen Co. Ltd.
>J. SMITHSON
>Secretary

Encl.

It happens fairly frequently that a customer deducts discount at a time when the invoice is due net. In such cases a polite letter has to be written, pointing out the reason why it cannot be allowed any more.

Weavewell Woollen Co. Ltd.
Victoria Street,
London, EC4X ISH

JS/EB 22nd February, 19—.
Messrs. Sampson & Hall Ltd.,
Staple House,
Cambridge Road,
Manchester, M4 9JO

Dear Sirs,

We acknowledge with thanks your cheque for £123.63 for which we enclose our official receipt.

You have deducted $2\frac{1}{2}\%$ discount, but we would point out that our invoice is dated 3rd December and discount could have been deducted only if payment had been made by 3rd January.

ACCOUNTS (2)

We are carrying the amount of £3.17 forward; would you please include it in your next remittance.

                    Yours faithfully,
                    p.p. Weavewell Woollen Co. Ltd.
                    J. SMITHSON
                    Secretary

Encl.

Another customer has made a mistake in calculating the discount and this is what Mr. Smithson writes:

              Weavewell Woollen Co. Ltd.
                  Victoria Street,
                London, EC4X ISH

JS/EB   23rd February, 19—.
Messrs. Dean & Stowe, Ltd.,
Dover Road,
Folkestone, CT6 3ND

Dear Sirs,

    We thank you for your cheque for £94.28 and have pleasure in enclosing our official receipt.

We should like to draw your attention to the error in the cash discount which you have taken. Our terms clearly state a discount of $2\frac{1}{2}\%$, and therefore the discount on our Invoice 9321 should read £2.46 and not £4.34. As there is a balance of £1.88 outstanding we should be obliged if you would kindly let us have this small amount with your next payment.

                    Yours faithfully,
                    p.p. Weavewell Woollen Co. Ltd.
                    J. SMITHSON
                    Secretary

Encl.

Exercises

I WORD STUDY. *Use the following:*

considerable, automatic, swell, interval, item, trace, due (also *overdue*), energetic (also *energy*), warning, ignore (use also *ignorant, ignorance*), solicitor, legal (use also *illegal*), reputation, dealings (= business; use *deal* also as a verb, 'to *deal with* a firm', i.e. do business with, 'to *deal in* woollen goods', i.e. to buy and sell, and as a noun, 'a business *deal*', i.e. a business transaction), confidence (use also *confidential, confidentially*), anticipate (and *anticipation*), integrity, justify, responsible (also *responsibility* and *irresponsible*), substantial, trustworthy, punctual, investigation (also *investigate*), efficient (also *efficiency* and *inefficient*), withdraw, contradiction, scrap, adjust (how does this differ from *justify*?), behalf (this word is used only in the phrases 'on our (your, my, etc.) behalf' and 'on behalf of' my firm (Mr. X, the company, etc.)).

II *Note the following technical words, phrases or sentences used in this chapter. Use each of them in sentences of your own:*
1. accounts are rendered quarterly; 2. settle the balance; 3. others pay after 60 days net; 4. the financial standing of the customer; 5. payment by return will oblige; 6. no trace, copy please; 7. we would remind you that; 8. please give this matter your attention; 9. let us have a cheque in settlement; 10. at an early date; 11. to receive your remittance by return; 12. we are unable to keep this account open any longer; 13. we must request you to let us have your cheque without delay; 14. we would point out that; 15. we trust you will give this matter your immediate attention; 16. our repeated applications for a settlement; 17. we have to inform you that; 18. we shall instruct our solicitors to take the necessary steps; 19. compelled to take legal proceedings; 20. whether a credit of £200 can be safely granted; 21. in strictest confidence; 22. thanking you in anticipation; 23. may we ask you to; 24. justify a credit of £200; 25. we shall be pleased to return the courtesy if occasion arises; 26. without responsibility; 27. liabilities have been met punctually and regularly; 28. to the best of our knowledge and belief; 29. cannot accept any responsibility; 30. make enquiries on our behalf; 31. the capital is insufficient for the large stock carried; 32. a writ was issued; 33. we would

ACCOUNTS (2)

advise great caution; 34. owing to a clerical error; 35. shown in our statement in error; 36. please find enclosed our corrected statement; 37. we are carrying this amount forward; 38. we have pleasure in enclosing our official receipt; 39. draw your attention to the error; 40. let us have this small amount with your next payment.

III *Write the following:*

1. A letter to Messrs. Carey & Brown, High St., Christminster, asking them to pay the balance of £26.83, now two months overdue.
2. A stronger letter to Carey & Brown a month later, as no reply has been received to the first letter.
3. A stronger and final letter to Carey & Brown who have ignored all previous reminders.
4. Messrs. Hayter & Small, Duke St., Glasgow, want to open an account with your firm. They give as reference The Glasgow Engineering Co., Bruce St., Glasgow. Write to the latter asking whether a credit of £350 would be justified.
5. Write a favourable reply from The Glasgow Engineering Co.
6. Write a letter of apology for an error in posting an invoice wrongly to a customer's account.
7. Write a letter to a firm pointing out that discount has been deducted from an invoice due net.
8. Write a letter to a firm pointing out that though the invoice was for £29.68, a cheque has by mistake been enclosed for £26.98.
9. Write to a customer telling him that owing to his constant unwillingness to settle his accounts promptly, you can do business with him in future only on a cash basis.
10. You settled an account three weeks ago. Now you have just received a statement of account for this. Write a letter explaining the position.
11. A firm has placed a large order but has made no reference to the terms of payment. Write a suitable letter.
12. Weavewell's paid an account of £345 two weeks ago to one of their suppliers, Messrs. Horrocks & Coates, Dunfermline, Scotland, but have not received an acknowledgment of the cheque, although they asked for one. Write an appropriate letter.

26
Statistics

Summary   Managing Director   chart   target

We have seen how purchases and sales of goods and the payments made and received are recorded in the books of the firm and built up into a great number of individual accounts. It is the work of the Statistical Department, which forms part of the Accounts Department, to collect, to group and to analyse all these figures in such a way as to give the management and the heads of the various departments a bird's eye view of the activities and the position of the company. Every month Mr. Smithson puts before the Managing Director a Summary which gives in a condensed form the information which is essential for the successful running of the business.

On the sales side the Summary shows the total of last month's sales, analysed into town, country and export sales, subdivided into areas and countries and grouped into articles and qualities. Other figures give the total of orders received during the month, split up into orders supplied from stock and orders for later delivery. The corresponding figures of last year are shown for comparison. A copy of these figures goes to the Sales Manager who can see at a glance whether they have gone up or down. An ambitious Sales Manager sets himself a target (i.e. the result he wants to achieve) and he can now easily check whether he has reached it. Mr. Austin translates the figures into lines by means of a chart which shows him graphically his position.[1]

Equally interesting and important is the information on the purchases side of the Summary. Orders given during the period, goods received in the month and the total of outstanding orders

---

[1] A chart is therefore often called a 'graph'.

are shown with the dates when these orders are due for delivery. All figures are again analysed in articles and qualities, and the Buyer of the firm, who receives a copy, knows from those figures exactly what his commitments are.

To the stock figure at the beginning of the month is added the amount of goods received; the sales (calculated at cost price) are deducted and the balance shows the stocks at the end of the month. The Managing Director will discuss this total with the Sales Manager and the Buyer if he feels that it needs adjustment.

The amount due from debtors is comparatively easily reckoned by adding the sales of the month to last month's total and deducting the payments received. In the same way the amount owed to suppliers can be worked out: invoices for goods received are added to the balance brought forward and payments made to suppliers are deducted from it. In this way, running balances of debtors and creditors are kept and these figures are, of course, carefully analysed according to the dates when they are due.

Like the captain of a ship who has to steer his vessel by looking at his chart,[1] at the stars, the weather reports and other information, the Managing Director decides the course of the business according to the picture the Summary shows him. If sales go down, special methods of vigorous sales promotion may be decided on and the limits for the Buyer will be reduced. If exports have fallen the reasons are examined to find whether there are perhaps any gaps in the overseas organisation, and an executive member of the firm may be sent out to put matters right. On the other hand rising sales and falling stocks call for a more active purchasing policy. When the figures show that money is coming in rather slowly, the Accounts Department is instructed to try to get it in more quickly. In short, the Summary,

---

[1] Note this other use of *chart*. We use *maps* on land, *charts* at sea.

'... if sales go down'

if intelligently read and interpreted, gives a clear record of progress and success or standstill and failure, and serves as a valuable guide to future action.

Exercises

I WORD STUDY. *Use each of the following:*

analyse ['ænəlaiz] (compare *analysis* [ə'næləsis]), 'a bird's eye view', area, ambitious (also *ambition* and *ambitiously*), target, achieve (also *achievement*), graphically (a *graph*), steer, chart (two meanings), vigorous, gaps, policy (use also *politics, political, police*), intelligent, interpret (also *interpreter, interpretation*), standstill.

II *In this chapter you have the sentences:*

'Every month Mr. Smithson *puts before* the Managing Director a summary.'

'An executive member of the firm may be sent out to *put* matters *right*.'

Note these other examples of the use of *put*.

Explain or translate them and make sentences of your own with them.

1. The meeting was *put off* till Friday.
2. Come and visit us; we shall be glad to *put you up* for a few days.
3. The Directors *put their heads together* to try to increase sales.
4. I made some enquiries about that firm and *putting two and two together* I wouldn't advise giving them credit.
5. Whatever *put the idea into your head* of going into business?
6. If this firm is to succeed, every member of it must *put his shoulder to the wheel*.
7. There has been considerable waste in the office, Mr. Smithson, we must *put a stop to* that.
8. I'll soon *put that right*.
9. The water soon *put the fire out*.
10. Conditions are not very satisfactory in the office, but we must just *put up with it*.
11. The firm has a large amount of capital *put away* in the bank.
12. The Sales Manager has *put in a lot of extra time* at his job.
13. There is an advertisement in the paper for an assistant manager; I am going to *put in for it*.
14. Henry was rather *put upon* by his older brothers.
15. 'Never *put off till tomorrow* what you can do today.' (Proverb.)

III *Answer the following:*

1. What work does the Statistical Department do?
2. What would you expect to find in a statistical summary?
3. What is the value of the Summary to (*a*) the Sales Manager; (*b*) the Buyer?

IV *Draw a chart on the basis of the following figures (in thousands of £):*

a. for sales last year and this year:

	JAN.	FEB.	MAR.	APRIL	MAY	JUNE
Last year	19	22	21	30	21	18
This year	24	26	27	18	30	27

b. for stock figures and purchases:

	I	II	III	IV	V	VI
Stock	184	156	131	178	124	114
Purchases	16	84	56	34	89	61

	VII	VIII	IX	X	XI	XII
Stock	169	178	136	144	130	118
Purchases	47	39	28	57	78	63

27
The Export Department

**house-phone   import quota   consul (consulate)
consular invoice   Certificate of Origin   foreign exchange
f.o.b.   c.i.f.   c. & f.   f.a.s.**

The house-phone rang on Mr. Smithson's desk. He picked it up and listened for a few moments. 'Yes, Mr. Clifford, he's here,' he said. . . . 'Very good, I'll send him up now. Thank you,' and he replaced the receiver. 'Petersen,' he said, 'Mr. Clifford wants to see you in his room now.'

Olaf was rather surprised; he had hardly spoken to the Manager since the first day he arrived, and as he made his way up to Mr. Clifford's room, he wondered vaguely whether anything was wrong. He needn't have worried; Mr. Clifford smiled as Olaf came in, pushed aside the papers on his crowded desk and said 'Good morning, Petersen, sit down. How are you liking Weavewell's?'

OLAF: Very much, sir.

MR. CLIFFORD: Learning a lot?

OLAF: Oh yes. I feel I really have quite a good general idea of the working of the firm.

MR. CLIFFORD: And you can write a business letter now?

OLAF: I think so; I've certainly seen plenty of examples.

MR. CLIFFORD: That's fine. I may say I have had good reports about you from the heads of all the departments that you have been in. They think you are hard-working and quite intelligent. (*He smiled and so did Olaf, looking a little confused.*)

But the hardest job is in front of you. You've been in all departments now except the Export, our most important one nowadays. You'll need all your hard work and intelligence to get a grip of the export trade. Luckily, Hammond's there—you know

Ben Hammond, our Export Manager, of course. If Hammond can't make the matter clear to you, no one can. I've had a chat with him and asked him to give you all the time he can spare and to do his best for you. That's all I wanted to say.

OLAF: Mr. Clifford, I can't say how grateful I am for the way you have treated me here. I ...

'That's all right, Petersen,' said Mr. Clifford, with a smile. 'Report to Hammond on Monday morning and he'll look after you. Good morning.'

Monday Morning

... 'Yes, Petersen,' said Mr. Hammond, 'I'm sure that this side of the business will interest you more than all the others, because that is what you will have to do one day. But I warn you: it is more complicated and you will sometimes find it a little confusing. I think I'll take one point at a time to give you a chance to digest what you have learned, and every time we have a talk together here I'll have with me one or two letters to illustrate each point.'

OLAF: Do you think it would perhaps be a good idea if I took a few notes of what you explain? I could then go through them and ask you about anything I have not quite understood.

MR. HAMMOND: Excellent idea. You see, there are so many points an exporter has to know; in fact, after two world wars and the havoc they have caused in international relations, it has almost become a science to find your way through all the official orders and regulations. The worst of it is that they are always changing. Countries which allowed imports without any difficulty yesterday may, today, impose restrictions in the form of import quotas or they may even stop imports altogether tomorrow; things like that sometimes happen even within close-knit economic communities such as our own E.E.C.[1] Another curse are the currency restrictions which often make it difficult

[1] E.E.C—European Economic Community, the 'Common Market'.

or even impossible to obtain payment from certain countries. Some countries require invoices to be certified by their consulate in London, what they call 'consular invoices'. Others demand certificates with the invoices showing the country of origin of the goods. On top of all that come the various forms required by the Bank of England to control all exports and dealings in foreign exchanges. But I don't want to confuse you now with all these details; if you want to, you can read them up in a book.[1] Many of these regulations are, we hope, only temporary; as a matter of fact, a lot of them have been scrapped in the last few years, and we can only hope that one day the world's monetary and currency problems will finally be solved. I think what you want is a short explanation of the essential and important points in which the terms and usages of the export trade differ from those in the home trade and which you must know wherever you are working in foreign trade.

OLAF: Well, I actually wanted to ask you a few things which I could not understand when I looked through some of the foreign letters. There was, for example, a letter from Das Gupta, Madras, asking for a quotation f.o.b. Liverpool. What does f.o.b. mean?

MR. HAMMOND: That is one of the terms used in quotations and offers in international trade which I want to explain now. You see, when you send goods overseas, several items which will affect the price have to be considered, for example packing, transport to the port, loading the goods on to the ship, etc. These expenses are difficult to calculate for a customer who is perhaps thousands of miles away. For that reason Das Gupta has asked for a quotation 'f.o.b. Liverpool', that means he wants our prices to include all charges until the goods are 'free on board' a vessel at Liverpool. All other expenses from there to Madras he has to pay.

[1] See *A Commercial Course for Foreign Students*, Vols. I and II.

OLAF: I suppose those would be mainly freight[1] charges.

MR. HAMMOND: Yes, and the cost of insurance, which is often quite considerable. But Das Gupta probably has his own insurance policy which covers all his shipments and he knows the freight charges between Liverpool and Madras. On the basis of an f.o.b. quotation he can therefore work out exactly what the goods will cost him 'landed Madras'.

OLAF: It seems a rather complicated calculation to me.

MR. HAMMOND: Yes, it is, and for that reason some firms ask us to send them a pro forma invoice first before they confirm an order. These pro forma invoices have to contain all the items which will be charged on the actual invoice. They are very convenient for the customer but they are a lot of trouble for us. Other firms ask for 'c.i.f.' quotations. In that case our prices have to include 'cost, insurance and freight' to the port of destination. Here is one, for example, 'c.i.f. Montevideo'. Is that clear to you?

OLAF: Oh yes, I understand that all right; as long as one remembers what the letters stand for one cannot really go wrong.

MR. HAMMOND: Well, that certainly helps. Now, here's one marked "c. & f." What do you think that means?

OLAF: It must mean 'cost and freight'; I suppose the importer in that case insures the goods himself.

MR. HAMMOND: You are quite right. It is, by the way, a quotation which many British importers prefer because they have good insurance facilities in London. There are a few more terms like f.a.s. (free alongside ship), etc., but f.o.b. and c.i.f. are the ones which you will meet most frequently. Now let's have a look at one or two letters of this kind: the first is an inquiry for an f.o.b. quotation from a customer in Madras, to which a reply with price list is sent; the second is a request from Salonika for a c.i.f. quotation, and this letter gives details of the method of payment proposed.

[1] *freight* [freit] = cost of transport.

Inquiry for f.o.b. quotation

Das Gupta & Company
14, Mount Road,
Madras

6th January, 19—.

Weavewell Woollen Co. Ltd.,
Victoria Street,
London, EC4X 1SH.

Dear Sirs,
 Please send us by return of post (air mail) patterns of tropical Frescoes[1] in grey, brown and light blue for delivery May/June; weight 300/350 g.

We have recently seen some material which was blended with Orlon or some other synthetic fibre, which seemed to us most suitable for our purposes. If you have any qualities of this type in your range we should be very interested indeed.

Kindly quote your best prices f.o.b. Liverpool.

>Yours faithfully,
>Das Gupta & Co.
>*P. RAH*
>Director

---

[1] Kind of cloth.

Reply

Weavewell Woollen Co. Ltd.
Victoria Street,
London, EC4X 1SH

BH/GK 1st February, 19—.

Messrs. Das Gupta & Co.,
14, Mount Road,
Madras.

Dear Sirs,

We thank you for your inquiry of 6th January and have pleasure in sending you herewith our range of tropical Frescoes in various colours.

All particulars are shown on the enclosed price list; our prices are f.o.b. Liverpool as requested.

From the labels on the patterns you will see that quality 61/104 consists of 100% Dacron and that 61/109 contains 75% Terylene and 25% wool. Both have sold extremely well and we can recommend them with confidence. The other qualities are pure wool.

There are now only a few firms who are making these special qualities, and as our supplies are limited we would advise you to place your order without delay.

Yours faithfully,
For Weavewell Woollen Co. Ltd.

B. HAMMOND
Export Manager

Air Mail
Encl.

PRICE LIST
Weavewell Woollen Co. Ltd.
Victoria Street,
London, EC4X 1SH

1st February, 19—.

Messrs. Das Gupta & Co.,
14, Mount Road,
Madras.

Quality	Width	Price	Delivery
Fresco			
61/104	175 cm.	£0.96	Apr./May
61/109	,,	£1.08	,, ,,
64/1, 2, 3	,,	£0.90	May/June
79/2, 4	,,	£1.34	,, ,,

F.O.B. Liverpool. Terms: Quarterly, 60 d/s.[1]

Inquiry for c.i.f. quotation

Alexander Metopoulos
Salonika

14th March, 19—.

Weavewell Woollen Co. Ltd.
Victoria Street,
London, EC4X 1SH

Dear Sirs,

We have a government inquiry for the supply of approx.[2] 15,000 metres Army Khaki. We enclose a pattern which will show you the shade and the quality required though the weight should be slightly less and not exceed 350 g.

---

[1] For explanation, see p. 209.   [2] *approx.* (approximately) = **about.**

Please send us by air mail your samples with best prices for pure woollen qualities which can be supplied within 8 weeks of placing the order. Kindly quote delivery c.i.f. Salonika, shipment by cargo liner.

Payment will be made by banker's draft[1] on arrival of the goods.

We shall be grateful if you will give this matter your immediate and careful attention.

                  Yours faithfully,

            ALEXANDER METOPOULOS

Encl.

Exercises

I WORD STUDY. *Use the following:*

vaguely, worry, intelligent (also *intelligence* and *unintelligent*), confused, nowadays, grip, chat, grateful (what is the corresponding noun?), digest (also *indigestion*), havoc, international, regulations (use also *regular*, *regularity*, *regulate*), impose (give the corresponding noun), restrictions (also *restrict*), curse (noun and verb), certify (also *certificate*), origin ['ɔridʒin] (use also *original* [ə'ridʒənl], affect (compare with *effect*), land (noun and verb), equal (verb and adjective; use also *unequalled*, *equalise*, *equality* [iː'kwɔliti]), facilities, tropical.

II *Explain the following:*

a) f.o.b., c.i.f., c. & f., f.a.s., an import quota, a consular invoice.
b) Which quotation is likely to be higher: f.o.b. or c.i.f.?

III *Note the following phrases used in Chapter 27. Use each in a sentence of your own:*

1. Orders and regulations; 2. impose restrictions; 3. currency restrictions; 4. certified invoices; 5. country of origin; 6. dealings in foreign exchanges; 7. a quotation f.o.b. Liverpool; 8. good

---

[1] See p. 203.

insurance facilities; 9. quote your best prices f.o.b. Liverpool; 10. terms quarterly.

IV *Write letters for the following:*

a) Daniels & Harris, Brisbane; enquire about toilet and household soap for prompt delivery, prices f.o.b. London.
b) Mackinnon & Miller, Cape Town; inquire for the exact price of 36 Herco bicycles. Ask for a pro forma invoice including all charges to Cape Town.

28
The Bill of Lading (B/L)

**Bill of Lading (B/L) terms of payment per S.S.
duplicate triplicate consignment open account
remit (remittance) sterling draft terms banker's draft
release documents advice title**

MR. HAMMOND: The next thing I want to explain to you is one of the most important documents in the export trade: the Bill of Lading (B/L). Perhaps I can make its use clear to you if I compare it with something that is familiar to you. I suppose you have often sent off a registered letter?

OLAF: Oh yes, many a time.

MR. HAMMOND: Now, when you post a registered letter the Post Office gives you a little slip. This slip is the acknowledgment of the receipt of the letter, and in return for the postage that you have to pay, the Post Office will deliver the letter to the person to whom it is addressed and will obtain his receipt. The Bill of Lading serves a similar purpose: on it the shipping company acknowledges the receipt of the goods to be shipped, and in return for the freight charge it undertakes to deliver the goods to the port and the person named on the bill. But there is one most important difference and I want you to keep that well in mind: before an importer can obtain delivery of the goods he must present one copy of the B/L. In other words the B/L is a title to the goods. It is made out in several copies, of which the exporter and the shipping company will keep one each for their records. In some cases one copy of the B/L will be sent direct to the customer; but more often the importer—that is, the customer—will only be able to get a copy in accordance with the terms of payment which have been agreed in the contract. You must remember this important point about the Bill of Lading, namely that without it the customer will not be able to get the goods. This safeguard for the exporter is used in the terms of payment which we must discuss now.

OLAF: How do the terms of payment in the export trade differ from those used in the home trade?

MR. HAMMOND: That depends on the customer we are dealing with and on the country to which the goods are sent. In many cases we allow our customers the same credit terms as in the home trade: we supply them on 'open account', send the usual monthly or quarterly statements and they remit in sterling, by banker's draft, that is a cheque drawn[1] by one bank on another. Naturally, we do that only where we are satisfied beyond doubt that the customer is sound and reliable, and where there are no currency restrictions which make payments difficult. In other cases we may ask for Cash with Order (C.W.O.) just as we sometimes do with doubtful customers in this country. Cash on Delivery (C.O.D.) is a little more difficult in exports. We use, of course, the postal C.O.D. services where possible, but for some countries the Post Office does not accept C.O.D. parcels, and in any case heavy goods cannot be sent by post. But we have a very good alternative: we hand the Bill of Lading to our bank with instructions to surrender it to the customer only against payment of our invoice. You remember that the customer cannot get the goods without the Bill of Lading; so he has, in fact, to pay C.O.D.

OLAF: That is clever; I see now the usefulness of the Bill of Lading.

MR. HAMMOND: Yes, but this is only one of the uses of the Bill of Lading and a comparatively rare one. The real value of the Bill of Lading is in connection with draft terms which are used in the export and import trade.

OLAF: Excuse me, Mr. Hammond, but what are draft terms?

MR. HAMMOND: Draft terms are those conditions of payment

[1] To *draw* a cheque or a bill means to write out a cheque or a bill.

under which the exporter draws a Bill of Exchange or, as it is very often called, a 'draft' on his customer or on a bank. But before we can examine the use of draft terms I must first explain to you what a Bill of Exchange is. Just look through those letters to illustrate what I have been talking about and then we'll go on to the Bill of Exchange.

'Open Account' terms

Weavewell Woollen Co. Ltd.
Victoria Street,
London, EC4X 1SH

BH/GK
A/B Larson & Dahl,
Stureplan 29,
Malmö.

22nd February, 19—.

Dear Sirs,

Your Order HY/4029

We thank you for your order of 18th February and enclose our invoice for £69.94.

The goods have been shipped today by S/S[1] 'Thames'; Bill of Lading in duplicate is enclosed.

We hope that this consignment will give you complete satisfaction and that you will have a ready sale for these goods.

Any further orders which you may place with us will receive our best attention.

Yours faithfully,
For Weavewell Woollen Co. Ltd.

B. HAMMOND

Export Manager

Encl.

---

[1] S/S (*or* S.S., or s.s.) = steamship.

THE BILL OF LADING

Documents against payment

Weavewell Woollen Co. Ltd.
Victoria Street,
London, EC4X 1SH

BH/GK   3rd March, 19—.
Messrs. Alfonso Rivada,
Serrano 24,
Barcelona.

Dear Sirs,
    We are pleased to tell you that the goods ordered by you on 26th Nov., 19—, have been shipped today by S/S 'Norwich' from Tilbury.[1]

We enclose commercial invoice in triplicate[2] for £124.64. As arranged we have handed the documents (Bill of Lading and Insurance Policy) to our bank, who will release them to you against payment of the amount of our invoice.

We are looking forward to your further orders.

                                    Yours faithfully,
                            For Weavewell Woollen Co. Ltd.

                                B. HAMMOND
                                Export Manager

Encl.

---

[1] A town on the Thames estuary with important docks.
[2] *Triplicate* ['triplikit] = three exact copies.

CHAPTER 28

Instructions to bank

Weavewell Woollen Co. Ltd.
Victoria Street,
London, EC4X ISH

BH/GK   3rd March, 19—.

The Manager,
West Midlands Bank Ltd.,
Old Broad Street,
London, EC20 ISC

Dear Sir,
    We enclose

                1 Invoice
                1 set Bills of Lading,
                1 Insurance Policy,

covering shipment per S/S 'Norwich' to Messrs. Alfonso Rivada, Serrano 24, Barcelona.

    These documents are to be surrendered against payment of £124.64, which please collect and credit to our account.

    We are awaiting your advice.

                          Yours faithfully,
                  For Weavewell Woollen Co. Ltd.

                          B. HAMMOND

                          Export Manager

Encl.

Exercises

I WORD STUDY. *Use the following:*

receipt [ri'si:t] (**note two meanings 1.** = document stating that money or goods have been received, e.g. 'Would you kindly let us have a receipt for our cheque for £26.66 sent on March

26th.' (*receipt* here is a common noun); 2. = the *receiving* of something, e.g. 'the shipping company acknowledges the receipt of the goods'. 'We are in receipt of your letter of 14th July' (*receipt* here is an abstract noun)), title (note the meaning in this chapter: 'The Bill of Lading is a *title* to the goods' = 'The Bill of Lading shows your right to possess the goods'), safeguard, 'in duplicate' = having two exact copies (what word would you use for 'three exact copies'?), alternative, assume (here = *suppose, take it for granted*), advice (note two meanings 1. = opinion and guidance; 2. = notification (as here, page 206)).

II *Show the difference in meaning and, where there is a difference, in pronunciation or accentuation between:*

1. *advice* and *advise*; 2. *practice* and *practise*; 3. *licence* and *license*; 4. *affect* and *effect*; 5. *import* (noun) and *import* (verb); 6. *export* (noun) and *export* (verb); 7. *separate* (adj.) and *separate* (verb); 8. *life* and *live*; 9. *whole* and *hole*; 10. *receipt* and *recipe*; 11. *present* (noun), *present* (adj.) and *present* [pri′zent] (verb).

III *Explain the following:*

Bill of Lading, per S/S, C.W.O., C.O.D., freight charge, terms of payment, credit terms, open account, draft terms.

IV *Write the following letters:*

a. Advise Kuomolainen & Co., Helsinki, Finland, that their order has been shipped by S/S *Bergen*. Enclose invoice £43.34 and ask for remittance. Enclose Bill of Lading and Insurance Policy.

b. Inform Messrs. Maron Fils, Cairo, that you have despatched 2 cases of cutlery. Enclose invoice for £136.90 and write that Bill of Lading has been handed to your bank who will surrender it against payment of invoice.

29
The Bill of Exchange (B/E)

Bill of Exchange (B/E)　　on demand　　at sight　　after sight
accept (acceptance)　sight bill　usance bill　documentary bill
documents against payment (D/P)
documents against acceptance (D/A)　　due dates
negotiate (negotiable)　　endorse　　to discount
banker's discount　　discount house　　overheads　　transaction
credit gap

MR. HAMMOND: I'll try to give you a definition of the Bill of Exchange in as simple terms as I can, leaving out all less important details. I think you ought to write this down:

'A Bill of Exchange is an order from a creditor to his debtor to pay on demand or at a given date a certain amount to the person named in the bill, or to his order.'

I know it sounds a little technical and complicated but as a matter of fact you have often drawn a Bill of Exchange yourself.

OLAF: No, Mr. Hammond, I am quite certain that I never have.

MR. HAMMOND: You have a banking account, haven't you?

OLAF: Yes.

MR. HAMMOND: Well, every cheque you draw is, in fact, a Bill of Exchange. Admittedly it is a special type of bill because it is always payable on demand and always drawn on a bank. But if you look at one of your cheques and compare it with the points I have given you, you will find that it agrees in every respect with my definition. Here is a cheque; now notice. It is an order given by you to your banker (who is your debtor) to pay on demand the amount you have filled in, to the person you want to pay, or to his order.

OLAF: So it is. I certainly didn't realise that when you gave me

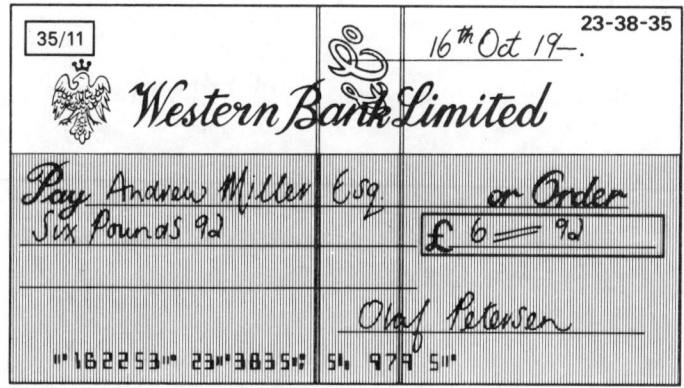

A cheque

the definition of a Bill of Exchange. You've made what seemed a complicated thing really quite clear and simple.

MR. HAMMOND: Thanks, but I am afraid my explanations are going to get a bit more difficult now. A cheque, as I said, is always payable on demand, but a foreign Bill of Exchange (and we are here concerned only with *foreign* bills) is payable either 'at sight', i.e. when it is presented to the debtor (a sight bill), or a certain number of days 'after sight' (a usance bill). So a draft may be payable 10 days after sight (10 d/s) or 30 days after sight (30 d/s) or 60 days after sight (60 d/s) or even at a later date.

OLAF: But how do you know whether you have to draw the bill at 30 or 60 or perhaps 90 days after sight?

MR. HAMMOND: That depends on the terms of payment which have been agreed between buyer and seller. If you look at our quotations or at an order which one of our agents sends from a new customer you will find that these terms are clearly noted, and if you look up foreign accounts in the export ledgers you will see that they are marked with these terms.

OLAF: There is another question. You said that the Bill of Exchange is an order to pay.

MR. HAMMOND: Yes, that's right.

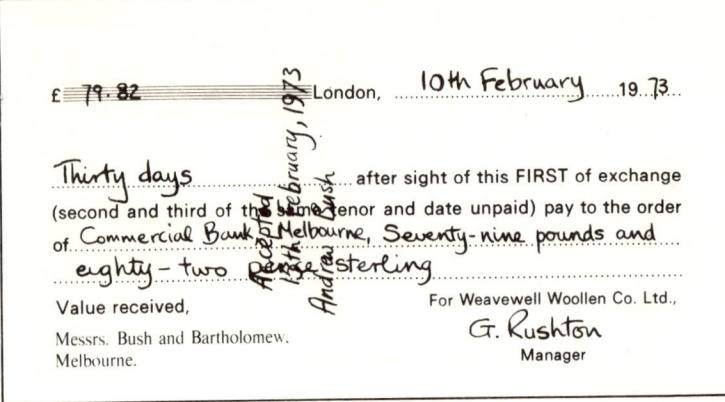

Bill of Exchange

OLAF: But the customer has not agreed that he will pay.

MR. HAMMOND: Well, every time we draw a bill we advise our customer by a short letter; he knows, therefore, that it will shortly be presented to him by the bank and that he will be asked to pay or to 'accept' it.

OLAF: How does he 'accept' a bill?

MR. HAMMOND: All the customer does is to sign his name across the face of a bill (which is now often called an 'acceptance'). By signing it he undertakes to pay the bill when it is due. If he doesn't, we say the bill has been 'dishonoured'. The bank will 'protest' the bill, that means obtain official proof that it has not been paid, and the customer will be in serious trouble.

DRAFT TERMS

MR. HAMMOND: Well, Olaf, so far we have discussed the use and the character of the Bill of Lading and the essential points of the Bill of Exchange. Do you think you have understood it all quite clearly?

OLAF: Yes, Mr. Hammond, I think so; if I haven't it's certainly not your fault; nobody could have put it more simply and concisely.

MR. HAMMOND: All right, we can then go on and examine the variations of draft terms which result from the different uses of the Bill of Lading and the Bill of Exchange. As I told you before, draft terms are all those conditions of sale which involve the drawing of a bill. They are flexible in order to allow the exporter and his overseas customer to choose the form which suits their individual requirements. The simplest form is explained easily. We allow our foreign customer credit terms similar to those allowed to a customer in the home trade; we send out our statement at regular intervals, as a rule quarterly, and draw a bill for the amount owing. This draft we give to our bank for collection and at the same time advise our customer in a short letter. Whether the bill will be payable at sight or 30 or 60 days after sight depends, as I said before, on the arrangements made with him.

OLAF: I suppose you do that only with old and established customers?

MR. HAMMOND: Quite right; we are now coming to those cases where we want to be more careful. And here we use what is called a 'documentary bill', that is to say we attach the bill to the shipping documents. There are two ways in which a documentary bill can be used. One way is to arrange that the documents, that is the Bill of Lading and the Insurance Policy, shall be handed to the customer only against payment of the Bill of Exchange; in that case we call the terms 'documents against payment' (D/P). The other way is to instruct the bank to surrender the documents against acceptance of our bill; in that case we speak of 'documents against acceptance' (D/A). You will notice the difference of credit in these terms?

OLAF: Yes, of course. When you surrender the documents only against payment of the bill you do not really risk anything.

MR. HAMMOND: Exactly. We can, of course, vary the terms still further by the 'due dates' of the bills, whether they are payable 'at sight' or at 3, 30, 60 or 90 days 'after sight'. Experience, recommendations by our agents, status inquiries, and references show us which terms are appropriate for each customer. But we may, of course, tighten or relax our terms if we find it necessary or advisable. For example, we may supply a new customer to begin with at 3 days after sight, documents against payment (3 d/s, D/P). Then, when we have done a considerable amount of business with him and found that he is all right we might grant him 60 days after sight and documents against acceptance (60 d/s, D/A). You see the difference, I hope.

OLAF: Oh yes. In the first case he has to pay almost immediately after presentation of the bill in order to get the documents and thereby the goods; in the second case he only has to accept the draft to get possession of the goods and he still has 60 days before he has to pay.

MR. HAMMOND: That's quite right, Olaf.

OLAF: But if you draw on your customer at 60 d/s or 90 d/s you have to wait a long time before you get your money.

MR. HAMMOND: Yes, in theory, but not in fact. There is one quality of the Bill of Exchange which I have not yet mentioned: a Bill of Exchange is 'negotiable'. That means that you can transfer it to somebody else by 'endorsing' it, and you do that by putting your signature on the back of the bill.

OLAF: But I still can't see how that helps you to get your money.

MR. HAMMOND: I'll soon make that clear. When you pay a cheque into your bank you are credited with the amount straight away, aren't you?

OLAF: Yes, but can the banks do that with a bill which is perhaps payable only in two or three months' time?

MR. HAMMOND: Oh yes, they can. When you endorse a bill to your banker, you sell it to him or, to use the technical term, you 'discount' it. There are in the City a number of banks, called 'discount houses', which specialise in purchasing bills. Of course, the buyer would want to know the credit standing of all the firms who have put their signature to the bill, but if he is satisfied, he will certainly buy it. The banker who buys it from you will credit you for it immediately but, believe me, he will debit you for it just as quickly if by any chance the bill is dishonoured. When you discount a bill the bank will deduct the interest for the time the bill has to run—the 'banker's discount', or commission. I hope I am not confusing you but you must remember that to *sell* a bill, to *negotiate* a bill, or to *discount* a bill all mean the same: you give up the ownership of it in favour of somebody else, usually a bank.[1]

OLAF: So the Bill of Exchange helps you in two ways: it gives you security and brings your money back quicker.

MR. HAMMOND: Yes, and that is a very important point. You see, the importer quite naturally wants long credits; the goods often take many weeks before they reach him, he has to market and sell them and then wait for his customer to pay him. The exporter, on the other hand, cannot afford to have a considerable part of his capital tied up in foreign accounts, he needs it to pay his suppliers, his overheads, and so on and he wants to use it again in new transactions. The Bill of Exchange is the instrument which bridges the 'credit gap' between buyer and seller and without it foreign trade could not work as it does in modern commerce. It is true that to a certain extent the Bill of Exchange has lost some of its importance and has been partly replaced by other credit instruments, for instance by Bank Transfers which I mentioned the other day and by the Letter of Credit which I'll try to explain to you next week. But before we do this, let's turn to the letters I have on my desk which illustrate what I have been telling you about Bills of Exchange.

---

[1] Actually the matter is more complicated still: to discount a bill also means to *buy* a bill. The banker who discounts a customer's bill buys it from him, but he may in turn discount (*sell*) it again to one of the big London discount houses.

CHAPTER 29

Letter with statement

Weavewell Woollen Co. Ltd.
Victoria Street,
London, EC4X 1SH

JS/EB 5th January, 19—.

Messrs. Bush & Bartholomew,
Lothian Place,
Melbourne.

Dear Sirs,

We enclose herewith the statement of your account showing a balance in our favour of £79.82.

We assume that you will remit by banker's draft on London but if you want us to draw on you please let us know.

Yours faithfully,
p.p. Weavewell Woollen Co. Ltd.

J. SMITHSON
Secretary

Encl.

'. . . you want us to draw on you'

THE BILL OF EXCHANGE

Advice of 30 d/s draft

Weavewell Woollen Co. Ltd.
Victoria Street,
London, EC4X 1SH

JS/EB
Messrs. Bush & Bartholomew,
Lothian Place,
Melbourne.

16th February, 19—.

Dear Sirs,

We acknowledge receipt of your letter of 24th January requesting us to draw on you for the balance of our December statement.

Accordingly we have today drawn on you at 30 d/s for the amount of £79.82 through the Commonwealth Bank of Australia, Melbourne. Please give our draft your protection.[1]

Yours faithfully,
p.p. Weavewell Woollen Co. Ltd.
J. SMITHSON
Secretary

---

[1] To 'protect' a bill means to pay it when it is due.

Quarterly terms, 60 d/s draft

Weavewell Woollen Co. Ltd.
Victoria Street,
London, EC4X 1SH

JS/EB 4th April, 19—.

Messrs. Das Gupta & Co.,
14, Mount Road,
Madras.

Dear Sirs,

Please find enclosed statement of your account for the quarter ended 31st March, 19—, amounting to £44.15.

Kindly note that we have drawn on you for this sum at 60 d/s. The bill will be presented through the Empire Bank, Madras, and we recommend it to your protection.

                    Yours faithfully,
              p.p. Weavewell Woollen Co. Ltd.

        J. SMITHSON
        Secretary

Encl.

Advice of shipment, 30 d/s, D/P

Weavewell Woollen Co. Ltd.
Victoria Street,
London, EC4X ISH

BH/GK   12th April, 19—.

Messrs. Lopez y Moya,
Triana 29,
Buenos Aires,
Argentine.

Dear Sirs,

We have pleasure in advising you that your order of 16th January has been shipped today by S/S 'Largo' from Avonmouth.

Please find enclosed our invoice for £231.72 and note that we have drawn on you for this amount at 30 d/s attaching the shipping documents (B/L in duplicate and Insurance Policy) to our draft.

As arranged, we have instructed our bank to give up the documents against payment of our draft which we recommend to your protection.

                         Yours faithfully,
                  For Weavewell Woollen Co. Ltd.

                          B. HAMMOND
                          Export Manager

Encl.

HEC

Request for better terms

Alfonso Rivada
**Serrano 24,
Barcelona**

14th March, 19—.

Weavewell Woollen Co. Ltd.,
Victoria Street,
London, EC4X 1SH

Dear Sirs,

Thank you for your letter of 3rd March, which arrived today.

We are pleased that you have been able to ship our order in good time but we are surprised that you still demand payment against documents. After several years of satisfactory trading we feel that we are entitled to easier terms. Most of our suppliers are drawing on us at 60 d/s, documents against acceptance, and we should be grateful if you could grant us the same terms.

Awaiting your reply,
We are,
Yours faithfully,
ALFONSO RIVADA

Letter granting 60 d/s, D/A

Weavewell Woollen Co. Ltd.
Victoria Street,
London, EC4X 1SH

JS/EB 21st March, 19—.

Messrs. Alfonso Rivada,
Serrano 24,
Barcelona.

Dear Sirs,

We have received your letter of 14th March in which you ask for an extension of our terms.

In consideration of the very pleasant business relationship we have had with your firm for several years, we have decided to agree to your suggestion. We shall, therefore, in future draw on you at 60 d/s, documents against acceptance, and trust that these terms will suit your requirements.

We hope that our concession will result in a considerable increase of your orders and assure you that we shall always endeavour to execute them to your complete satisfaction.

Yours faithfully,
p.p. Weavewell Woollen Co. Ltd.

J. SMITHSON
Secretary

Exercises

I WORD STUDY. *Use the following:*

admittedly (use also *to admit* with two meanings), variations (use also *vary*, *variable*, *invariable*), flexible (use also *flexibility*, *inflexible*), surrender, appropriate (adj. There is also a verb *to appropriate* = to take over or to allocate for a special purpose), tighten (use also *tight*), relax (also *relaxation*), transfer (noun and verb), ownership, entitled (compare with *title*, page 202), concession (the corresponding verb is *to concede*), execute (also *execution*; note the two meanings of this word).

II *Note the form:*

You have a banking account, *haven't you*? We very often ask a question in this way, i.e. by making a statement and adding a 'question phrase'.[1] Add the right question phrases to the following:

1. You have met Mr. Clifford, —— ?
2. He has signed the letter, —— ?
3. You can understand that, —— ?
4. He could pay the money, —— ?
5. You will pay the money, —— ?
6. I shall get the money, —— ?
7. That point is quite clear, —— ?
8. Those cheques were signed, —— ?
9. He must alter the figures, —— ?
10. We ought to sign that, —— ?
11. You understand that, —— ?
12. The ship sails from Tilbury, —— ?
13. I sign the Bill of Exchange here, —— ?
14. Brown and Cookson always pay their accounts promptly, —— ?
15. I made a mistake then, —— ?
16. You understood that, —— ?
17. The ship sailed on Friday, —— ?
18. Brown & Cookson paid their account, —— ?
19. Brown & Cookson have paid their account, —— ?
20. Mr. Clifford wrote the letter, —— ?
21. Mr. Clifford will write the letter, —— ?

[1] See *Essential English I*, pp. 223-4 and 233-4.

22. Mr. Clifford has written the letter, ——— ?
23. Mr. Clifford is writing the letter now, ——— ?

III Give the definition of a Bill of Exchange. How does a cheque resemble a Bill of Exchange? How does it differ from it?

IV *Explain the following:*
B/E; 30 d/s; D/P; D/A; 60 d/s D/A.

V *Answer the following:*

1. How are foreign Bills of Exchange payable? 2. Where are terms of payment noted? 3. How does a customer 'accept' a Bill? 4. What does a bank do if a customer does not pay a bill? 5. What are draft terms? 6. Why are draft terms flexible? 7. What is the simplest form of draft terms? 8. To whom do you give the draft for collection? 9. How does the customer know about this? 10. What is meant by a documentary bill? 11. In what two ways can a documentary bill be used? 12. Why will a firm prefer D/A to D/P? 13. Give examples to show how you can vary the terms by the 'due dates' of bills. 14. What considerations would guide you in fixing the due dates of bills? 15. If you were an importer would you prefer a bill marked '3 d/s, D/P' or one marked '60 d/s, D/A'? Why? 16. How do you 'endorse' a Bill of Exchange? 17. What is meant by 'discounting' a bill? 18. What is 'banker's discount'? 19. In what two ways does a Bill of Exchange help (*a*) an exporter, (*b*) an importer? 20. What do you understand by the 'credit gap'?

VI *Write the following letters:*

a. Send your quarterly statement to your customer in Lima, Peru, and advise him that you have drawn on him at 30 d/s through the Bank of Peru; ask for protection of your bill.

b. Write to a customer in Auckland, N.Z., and inform him that you have changed your terms from 30 d/s D/P, to 90 d/s D/A.

30
The Letter of Credit (L/C)

**non-acceptance   non-payment   sue   Letter of Credit (L/C)
branch   irrevocable   cancel   valid
Documentary Letter of Credit**

OLAF: Mr. Hammond, I have read through the notes I took yesterday about draft terms. They really seem to cover almost every point. But I still see one difficulty that might arise: what happens when you have sent goods abroad against a customer's order and he refuses to accept or to pay your documentary bill? I know he cannot get the goods but perhaps he does not want them any more for one reason or another. What do you do in such a case?

MR. HAMMOND: That was a good question, Olaf. I can see we are going to make a first-rate business man of you before we finish. Yes, there is that danger, of course, and it creates a very unpleasant situation. We might try to sell the goods to another customer in the same area or even let him have them on a 'see-safe'[1] basis. But this is, of course, not always possible. On the other hand it would be very expensive to have the goods returned to us from perhaps 3,000 miles away; so we would first ask the bank to present the bill again and we would write to our customer and request him to fulfil the contract. If he refused again we would instruct the bank to protest the bill for non-acceptance or non-payment and could then take legal action. But to sue a firm in a foreign country is a lengthy, costly and doubtful matter. For this reason we, and all experienced exporters, are very cautious in dealing with orders from new customers. If a firm is unknown to us or if we have the slightest doubt about

---

[1] '*see-safe*' = on sale or return.

THE LETTER OF CREDIT

'... on a "see-safe" basis'

its financial standing we don't despatch the goods unless we are assured of payment by a 'Letter of Credit'.

OLAF: I remember, I had a Letter of Credit when I arrived in England two years ago. My father had arranged it with his bankers in Stockholm before I left and I was able to draw certain amounts from their branch in London; all I had to do was to sign a form.

MR. HAMMOND: You had a 'Traveller's Letter of Credit'; the commercial Letter of Credit which is used in international trade is similar. Your father had arranged with his bankers to hold a certain amount of money at your disposal at their London branch against your signature. If one of our customers provides us with a Letter of Credit (L/C) he arranges that his bankers or their house in London shall pay us the amount of our invoice. Or—and that happens more frequently—he may instruct them to accept a B/E which we draw on them. These instructions are confirmed to us by the bank and we know, therefore, that we shall either receive payment or have our draft accepted by a bank. Usually it is a condition of the credit that the documents relating to the shipment shall be handed over against payment or against acceptance of the draft; we then speak of a 'Documentary Letter of Credit', similar to the 'Documentary Bill of Exchange' which I mentioned the other day.

Such an arrangement suits us, of course, very well because it excludes practically every risk. But it has advantages for the customer too. Without the Letter of Credit we would probably have asked for Cash with Order. Now he need only pay when the goods are ready for shipment or, in the case of a draft, at maturity of the bill. For these reasons, the Letter of Credit is becoming more popular every year and it is now very widely used. You will see that we are very often asking new customers to provide us with such an instrument before we accept or execute their orders.

Let me explain how it works in practice; you will probably find it easier to follow.

Our agent in Venezuela has sent us an order from Miguel Fernandos in Caracas for about £800. As we do not know this customer, and he wants the goods to be shipped as soon as possible, it has been agreed that payment shall be made by Letter of Credit. By the way, we always demand that the credit shall be 'irrevocable', that means that the bank cannot cancel it.

Now first of all Fernandos goes to his bankers, the City Bank of Caracas, and instructs them to open an 'Irrevocable Letter of Credit' for £800 in our favour through their agent in London. Banking houses all over the world either have their own branch here or have made arrangements with a London bank to act as their agents or correspondents. In the instructions to his bank Fernandos must give exact details of the terms and conditions of the credit:

a. the amount (£800)

b. the period for which it shall be valid (until 30th September, 19—)

THE LETTER OF CREDIT

c. the particulars of the shipment which is to be covered by the credit (20 pieces of approx. 50 yds. each, worsted flannels)

d. the terms of the draft (in this case 60 days after sight)

e. the documents which are required (Bill of Lading, Insurance Policy, Consular Invoice)

The City Bank of Caracas, which has known Miguel Fernandos for many years, accepts these instructions and passes them on to its agent in England, the Central American Trust Co. in London.

This bank, on receipt of these instructions, will send us a letter confirming that it is prepared to accept our draft if it is drawn in strict accordance with these terms. That is, of course, exactly what we want: we draw our bill at 60 d/s on the Central American Trust Co. in London, hand it with the documents to our bankers and instruct them to surrender the documents against acceptance of the bill.

OLAF: I think I have followed you all right, but it is certainly a complicated business to open a Letter of Credit.

MR. HAMMOND: It is not quite so difficult as it may seem to you. You see, when Miguel Fernandos goes to the bank and tells them that he wants to issue a credit to a firm overseas, the City Bank will provide him with a standard form which it has prepared for such cases and all Fernandos has to do is to read it carefully, to fill it in and to sign it (see page 228).

OLAF: You know, the more you tell me about the methods of modern commerce the more I realise how clever they are and how well they can be adapted to so many and such varied purposes.

MR. HAMMOND: Oh, there's lots more I could tell you, but you have got at least the general outline of the export trade. You'll find quite a good bit more in that book I told you about a day or two ago.[1] There are just one or two more letters and documents I've got for you here—and then you can start and do a bit of work in the department.

[1] See footnote, p. 195.

Confirming an order against Letter of Credit

Weavewell Woollen Co. Ltd.
Victoria Street,
London, EC4X 1SH

BH/GK 2nd June, 19—.

Messrs. Miguel Fernandos y Cia.,
Caracas,
Venezuela.

Dear Sirs,

Your Order TE/1614

We acknowledge with thanks the receipt of your order which reached us through our representative, Mr. Charles Kendal. The goods which you have ordered are being prepared for shipment.

Mr. Kendal has informed us that you will arrange payment by Irrevocable Letter of Credit in our favour, to be valid until 30th September, 19—.

As soon as the credit has been confirmed the goods will be packed and shipped in accordance with your instructions.

Please be assured that all your orders will have our most careful attention.

Yours faithfully,
For Weavewell Woollen Co. Ltd.

B. HAMMOND

Export Manager

By Air Mail.

Advice of L/C

Miguel Fernandos y Cia
Caracas

18th June, 19—.

Weavewell Woollen Co. Ltd.,
Victoria Street,
London, EC4X 1SH

Dear Sirs,

With reference to your letter of 2nd June we write to inform you that we have instructed the City Bank of Caracas to open a credit for £800 in your favour, valid until 30th September, 19—.

This credit will be confirmed by the Central American Trust Co. in London and will be available by your draft on this bank at 60 d/s.

Please attach the documents, i.e.

    Bill of Lading in duplicate
    Insurance Policy for £880[1]
    1 Consular Invoice
    5 Commercial Invoices

and surrender them against acceptance of your bill.

                We are awaiting your advice,
                  and remain,
                  Yours faithfully,
                  MIGUEL FERNANDOS Y CIA.

Air Mail.

---

[1] It is usual to insure shipments at 10% or 15% over invoice value.

Instruction Form to open L/C (simplified)

The Manager,
  City Bank,
    Caracas.

Dear Sirs,
    We request you to open by cable an Irrevocable Documentary Credit in favour of
    Weavewell Woollen Co. Ltd.
    Victoria Street, London, EC4X 1SH

for the amount of £800 (eight hundred pounds sterling) available by draft at 60 (sixty) d/s on your agent in London.
  The following documents are required:

    Bills of Lading in duplicate.
    Insurance Policy for £880.
    Consular Invoice.
    5 Commercial Invoices.
    to evidence shipment of 20 pieces of
    approx. 50 yds. each of worsted flannels.

 The Credit is to be confirmed to
Weavewell Woollen Co. Ltd. as above
and shall cease to be valid after
    30th Sept. 19--.
 Special instructions: Documents to be forwarded to us by Air Mail.

                            Yours faithfully,
                            MIGUEL FERNANDOS Y CIA.
    Caracas, 18th June, 19--.

THE LETTER OF CREDIT

Exercises

I WORD STUDY. *Use the following:*

branch, correspondents (don't confuse with *correspondence*), valid (negative, *invalid* [in'vælid]. Note the other word *invalid* ['invəli:d], meaning 'a person who is ill'), 'in strict accordance with', adapt (compare with *adopt*).

II *Complete the following by adding 'question phrases' (Be careful with the intonation when saying the phrases aloud):*

1. You haven't met Mr. Clifford —— ?
2. He hasn't signed the letter —— ?
3. You can't understand that —— ?
4. He couldn't pay the money —— ?
5. You won't pay the money —— ?
6. I shan't get the money —— ?
7. That point isn't quite clear —— ?
8. Those cheques weren't signed —— ?
9. He mustn't alter those figures —— ?
10. They needn't pay at once —— ?
11. We oughtn't to sign that —— ?
12. You don't understand that —— ?
13. The ship doesn't sail from Tilbury —— ?
14. Brown & Cookson don't always pay their accounts promptly —— ?
15. I don't sign the Bill of Exchange here —— ?
16. I didn't make a mistake then —— ?
17. You didn't understand that —— ?
18. The ship didn't sail on Friday —— ?
19. Brown & Cookson didn't pay their account —— ?
20. Brown & Cookson haven't paid their account —— ?
21. Mr. Clifford didn't write the letter —— ?
22. Mr. Clifford won't write the letter —— ?
23. Mr. Clifford hasn't written the letter —— ?
24. Mr. Clifford isn't writing the letter now —— ?

III 1. What action would you take if a customer refused to accept or to pay a bill?
2. How can you prevent this difficulty from arising?
3. What is a Letter of Credit?

4. What is meant by a Letter of Credit being 'irrevocable'?
5. What details must you give to a bank concerning the terms and conditions of a credit?
6. What is a 'Documentary Letter of Credit'?
7. What are the advantages of a Letter of Credit:
   (a) for the seller; (b) for the buyer?

IV a. Imagine you are a merchant in Lima. You want a Letter of Credit for £700 to pay for goods you want to order from London. Explain exactly what you must do.
b. Inform your customer in Teheran that the order he has given you will be ready for shipment in 4 weeks. Ask him to open a Letter of Credit (irrevocable) for £300 in your favour against shipping documents.
c. Draft the reply from the customer in Teheran, saying that an irrevocable documentary credit has been issued in your favour through the Bank of Iran who will accept a 30 d/s bill against the following documents:

Bill of Lading (3)
Insurance Policy (£330)
Consular Invoices (2)
Commercial Invoices (4)

Conclusion

Olaf writes a letter home.

Anglo-Swedish Club,
Piccadilly,
London, W1L 9FC
21st October, 19—.

Dear Father,

I have now spent a year at Weavewell's, one of the most interesting and, I think, one of the most useful years of my life. When I first went into their office I hardly knew the difference between an invoice and a Bill of Lading—in fact I didn't know there were such things as Bills of Lading. Now invoices, statements, Letters of Credit, Bankers' Drafts, f.o.b., etc. etc., are all familiar friends. I can write a business letter, apply for a job, post accounts, make a telephone call or negotiate a Bill of Exchange without getting too worried about it.

I can never be sufficiently grateful for all that Weavewell's have done for me. I have been through all the departments, the General Office, the Sales Department, the Warehouse, Invoice and Accounts Department and the Export Branch. And in every case I have made a special study of the correspondence and documents of the department: incidentally, I have learned a great deal more *English* as well as *Commerce*.

I have been greatly impressed by the quiet efficiency of the firm but even more by the kindness of everyone I met—Mr. Clifford, Mr. Austin, George Brown, Mr. Smithson, Ben Hammond—all of them from the General Manager down to the telephonist and office boy did everything they could to explain the work to me and help me to understand it. I am leaving the firm tomorrow and my ship sails for home next Thursday. I am looking forward very much to seeing you all again, but I'm feeling a bit sad at leaving these friends here—for they have become real friends. I've invited them all to come and visit us in Sweden. I hope they will come (not all of them at the same time, of course!). I'm sure you will like them as much as I do.

I'll send you a telegram later to let you know the time my ship is due into Gothenburg.[1]

Till then love and all good wishes,

OLAF

---

[1] Olaf really wrote *Göteborg*; the usual English form is *Gothenburg*.

Appendix I
Standard Phrases for Correspondence

In this selection we have not attempted to give every variation of phrase that the student may require for the writing of business letters; if we had, the result would probably have confused him more than helped him. Nor is it the aim of this appendix to enable the student to write letters by picking out phrases and putting them together like a jigsaw puzzle. We want him to use his intelligence and the knowledge of English and Commerce that we have tried to give him in this book. We hope, however, that this selection will help him, when doubts arise, to find the right expression.

The Appendix follows, roughly, the same grouping as the chapters in this book, i.e. Inquiries, Quotations, Orders, Complaints, etc. Frequent reference to the numerous examples of correspondence in the text will be useful.

In most sections we have given

a) some appropriate opening phrases;
b) an indication of the subject matter;
c) details, terms, instructions, etc.;
d) suitable endings.

Most of the phrases are arranged in two columns. Any phrase in the left-hand column can, within the context of the letters, be used with any phrase in the opposite right-hand column. By the intelligent use of the various combinations, a wide variety of letters can be built up, dealing with all the main aspects of Commercial Correspondence, and the student will be able to write letters that are at once personal, effective and correct.

Inquiries

a) Please (Kindly) send us
 We shall (should) be pleased (grateful, obliged) if you will (would) send us
 We shall be glad to receive
} your price list (catalogue, patterns, samples, range) of . . . with your lowest prices

 We have an inquiry for . . .
 We require . . .
 We are interested in . . .
 We are in the market for . . .
 We have seen your advertisement in . . .
 We have seen your stand at the . . . Trade Fair
} and would ask you to send us (and would be obliged if you would send us) your price list (etc.) with your best terms.

b) Please offer qualities (articles, goods)
 Please send us samples (patterns) of . . .
 We are only interested in goods
} which you can supply from stock (for prompt delivery, for delivery Jan./Feb., etc.) which can be shipped within . . . weeks from receipt of order.

 We should be grateful if you would quote (Please quote) } f.o.b. London (c.i.f. New York, f.a.s. Liverpool).

c) If your prices (terms, qualities) are satisfactory (competitive, attractive) } we shall (may) send you (place) an order (a trial order, a substantial order, regular orders).

 We shall supply (give, submit) the usual trade references (bank and trade references, first class references) with our order (if we place an order).

d) Your immediate attention will oblige

 We look forward to having your reply } as soon as possible (by return, by air mail).

 An early reply will oblige

Offers

a) Thank you for your letter of . . .
We thank you for your letter (inquiry) of . . .
We acknowledge with thanks . . .
We are obliged for your letter (inquiry) of . . .

b) As requested
With reference to your inquiry
In reply to your letter

we are sending you herewith (under separate cover) we have pleasure in sending you we enclose	our latest (illustrated) catalogue (our price list, our spring list, our winter list, our range of patterns, a good selection of samples of . . .)

All details (particulars) are shown (given) in our price list (catalogue).
We have quoted our best (lowest) prices on the enclosed price list.
Our offer is without commitment (subject to the goods being unsold on receipt of your order).
All prices are subject to alteration without notice.
We can deliver from stock (at once, within . . . weeks).
We are at present accepting orders for delivery in . . . months (for delivery Sept./Oct., etc.).
Our quotation includes delivery f.o.b. London (c.i.f. Smyrna, f.a.s. Liverpool).

c) *Terms:* Usual Terms, Terms as before, Net, Strictly Net, Cash with Order (C.W.O.) on new accounts, Cash on Delivery (C.O.D.).
Payable 10th of following month less $2\frac{1}{2}\%$.
30 days 5%, 60 days $2\frac{1}{2}\%$, 90 days net.

Export Terms:
Payment by Bank Draft on London against Pro Forma Invoice.
Documents against payment (D/P).

Documents against acceptance of our 30 days' sight draft.
Shipping documents will be surrendered against Irrevocable Letter of Credit.
Quarterly 30 days' sight (d/s).
Monthly 60 days' sight.

---

d) We hope (We trust, We are confident) that you will find the article (the goods) you want in our range (catalogue) and are looking forward to receiving your order.

Please let us know if our offer does not contain what you require (want); we shall be glad to send you further samples.

As prices are rising
As our stocks are rather low } we would advise you to order
As we are booking heavy orders every day } soon (by return).

We shall be pleased to receive your order, and remain,
Any order which you may place with us will have our prompt and careful attention. } Yours faithfully,

---

Orders

---

a) We thank you for
We refer to
We acknowledge with thanks
} your letter (offer, quotation) of . . . with price list (catalogue, patterns, samples).

---

b) Please supply (send us) by post (rail, passenger train, next boat, air mail) . . .

Please book the following order:

We have pleasure in enclosing our Order No. . . .
We enclose herewith our Order No. . . .
} with detailed instructions (for your (best, prompt) attention).

We require } immediate (prompt, punctual) delivery
Please arrange for } (despatch, shipment).

The goods are required at once (immediately, within . . . weeks).

The order must be despatched (executed) without delay (not later than . . .)

We shall not accept delivery (goods arriving) after . . .

The delivery dates (instructions) given in our order must be strictly kept (adhered to).

Please despatch (deliver, ship, pack, mark) in strict accordance with our instructions.

We expect (await) delivery at the specified dates.

The goods must comply (agree) in every respect with our specifications (with the samples, patterns).

Please do not supply substitutes.

Please choose nearest substitute for any article out of stock.

---

c) Please advise us when the order is ready for delivery (shipment).

Detailed (Full) instructions regarding marks and numbers (packing, shipping route) will follow.

Please await our instructions for insurance.

Please insure at invoice value plus 10% (15%, 20%).

We shall take out (effect, cover) insurance here (ourselves).

Please quote our Order No. (the above Order No.) on all letters and invoices (documents).

We require invoice in duplicate (triplicate, quadruplicate, with 5 copies) and two consular invoices (certificates of origin).

As this is our first order (our first transaction with you) {
 we shall remit on receipt of your pro forma invoice.
 we enclose cheque (bank draft) for £100.
 we give you the following references:
 Messrs. . . . .
 Messrs. . . . .
}

If your goods are satisfactory we may be able (we hope) to place substantial orders (repeat orders).

d) Please give (We hope that you will give) our order your prompt and careful attention.

We shall appreciate your careful attention to our instructions.

We expect careful (prompt, speedy) execution of our order.

Kindly acknowledge (confirm your acceptance of) our order by return of post (by air mail, cable).

Please inform us whether you can accept our order on these terms.

We are awaiting your confirmation (copy order, illustrated copy order) by return (of post).

Acknowledgment and Execution of Orders

a) We thank you (are obliged for) / We are in receipt of (have received) / We acknowledge with thanks (are pleased to acknowledge) } your order of ... (your order No. ....) which is having (receiving) our best attention (which we confirm as follows:)

Your order No. ..., for which we thank you, has been booked as instructed and we enclose (have pleasure in enclosing) herewith our confirmation (copy order, illustrated copy order).

---

b) Please note (we are pleased to advise (inform) you) that the goods (pieces, articles) } have been despatched today. / are now ready for delivery. / will be ready for despatch (shipment) next week.

We enclose (attach) / Enclosed please find / We are sending you herewith (we attach) / Please find enclosed (attached) } our invoice for £ ... (to the amount of £ ...) / invoice and Bill of Lading in duplicate with Insurance Policy. / invoice in triplicate, consular invoice in duplicate and Insurance Policy.

c) Please let us have (send us) / We are awaiting / Your order is now complete (ready for shipment) and we shall be pleased (glad) to receive by return — your shipping instructions. / your instructions as regards marks and numbers (packing, insurance).

As instructed (requested) we have effected insurance and will attach the policy to the shipping documents.

We have noted that you are covering insurance yourselves (from your side).

We regret (We are sorry) that No. .... is sold out.

Please select (choose) a suitable substitute (another article, quality) from the enclosed patterns (samples, from our catalogue).

For No. .... which is out of stock at present we have substituted the very similar article... at the same price and hope (trust) that you will agree (approve).

The rest of your order will follow shortly (soon, next month, as soon as possible).

d) We hope (We shall be pleased) to receive your further orders which shall always have our best attention.

We trust (are confident) that you will find a ready sale for this excellent quality and are looking forward to your further orders (repeat orders).

Please be assured that we shall spare no effort to satisfy your wishes (requirements).

Any future order which you may place with us will be handled with the greatest care and attention.

References

I. *Inquiries*

a) Messrs. A. N. Other & Co. of Alltown have given us your name (firm) as a reference.

We have received an order from Messrs. A. N. Other & Co. of Alltown.

b) May we ask you / Would you be good enough
- to give us some information about their financial standing (reputation, reliability).
- to let us know whether a credit up to £100 can in your opinion be safely given (granted).

Please let us know / We are especially interested to know
- whether your dealings with them have always been satisfactory.
- whether they have always met their commitments punctually (promptly).

c) Your information / Any information you may be able to give will be treated in strict confidence (strictly confidentially).

d) We thank you in anticipation and / Thanking you in advance we enclose stamped, addressed envelope (an International Reply Coupon) for your answer (reply).

II. *Replies*

a) We are in receipt of your letter of ... / We write in reply to your letter of ... / We refer to your inquiry of — and give you below the information you require (you have asked for).

b) *favourable*

The firm you mention (in question) / The firm about which you inquire / Messrs. A. N. Other & Co. of Alltown
- have been regular customers of ours (have had an account with us) for many years.
- have always met their commitments promptly (without delay, satisfactorily).
- are well-established dealers of the highest repute.

We think	that a credit of £100 can be granted (given, recommended) with confidence (without risk).
We are of the opinion	
We have no hesitation in saying	

---

c) *unfavourable*

The firm whose name is shown on the enclosed slip	is unknown to us.
The firm about which you inquire	is a new (recent) customer.
	has only a very small account with us.
	has been rather slow in its payments.

| We regret that we are unable | to give you (supply) the information you require (need, want). |
| We feel that we do not know them well enough (sufficiently well) | |

We are not in a position to recommend	a credit of £100 (of the amount you mention).
We would be reluctant to grant	
We would hesitate to advise	

We would advise the greatest caution.
We would supply on a cash basis only.

---

d) This information is given in strict (absolute) confidence.
   We give this information in strict confidence and without responsibility.
   This information is given in strict confidence and without any responsibility on our part.

Collection of Accounts

First Application

We enclose herewith our monthly (quarterly) statement. We refer to the statement of account which we sent you last month. With reference to our letter of . . . asking for payment of the overdue balance of £. . . .	We shall be pleased to receive your cheque (remittance) by return (at an early date). We would appreciate (be grateful for) an early settlement (payment by return).

Second Application

We wrote to you on . . . regarding our overdue account On . . . we called your attention to our account of £ . . .	and would ask you to give this matter your immediate attention (to remit this amount (balance) by return of post).

Third Application

We must remind you again of our overdue account We are still without payment of our long overdue account We regret that you have ignored our previous applications for a settlement of our account	and must request you to let us have your payment (cheque, remittance) without further delay (by return of post, at once).

Final Application

As our previous applications for payment have been without result As you have not replied to three letters asking for a settlement of the overdue balance of our account No replies to our letters of . . . and . . . having been received,	we shall have to place the matter in other hands unless we receive payment within 7 days. we shall take legal proceedings (instruct our solicitors) if your remittance has not reached us by the . . . th of this month.

Export Accounts

We enclose herewith our statement (invoice) amounting to £6.29.	Kindly let us have your cheque (draft) in settlement. May we ask you to remit, as we do not want to draw for this small amount.
Please find enclosed our invoice for £25.85 covering your order No. . . . . We have pleasure in sending you herewith our December statement showing a balance due of £68.16.	We would advise you that we have drawn on you at 30 d/s through the Bank of South Africa. Please give our draft your kind (due) protection.
We are pleased to advise you that your order No. . . . has been shipped today (is ready for shipment). Enclosed please find our invoice for £126.69 which we trust you will find in order.	The shipping documents will be delivered (surrendered) against payment (acceptance) of our draft which we recommend to your protection. As agreed (arranged) we would ask you to open an irrevocable credit in our favour and shall hand over shipping documents against acceptance of our draft.

As requested (arranged) we are sending you pro forma invoice. The goods will be despatched on receipt of payment (remittance).

Complaints

I. *Delays*
a) We refer to our letter of . . . (telephone call, telegram, cable of today).

STANDARD PHRASES FOR CORRESPONDENCE 243

b) Our order No. .... of ...
   The goods we ordered on ...
   As we pointed out, our order
} is (are) now considerably (long) overdue.
should have been delivered (despatched, shipped) on ... (last month, 4 weeks ago).

---

c) As the goods are urgently needed (required)
   As the goods are required (wanted) for next month's sales (for Christmas, for Easter, for Whitsun)
} we must ask (request) you to despatch them without further delay (by return).
we must now insist on immediate delivery (shipment, execution) of our order.

As these goods (articles, qualities) were specially ordered for the spring (autumn) season
As the demand for these qualities has now ceased
Unless the goods can be despatched (shipped) immediately (at once, within .... days)
} we have to (must) ask you to cancel our order (contract).

---

d) Please give this matter your immediate (urgent) attention.
   Please let us know (inform us) by return (by telegram, cable) when we can expect delivery.
   We are expecting your reply (confirmation, advice) by return of post.

II. *Goods unsatisfactory or damaged*

a) We refer to our Order No. .... (to your invoice, Advice Note of ...).

---

b) The goods have arrived (been delivered) today.
   The consignment (The shipment, The bale, The case, The crate, The parcel) has been received (delivered) today.

c) When unpacking the bale (case, etc.) we found that On examination we found that We were surprised to find that	the colour (weight, finish) is unsatisfactory. the goods do not agree with the original pattern. the quality is inferior to that of the sample. the contents do not tally (agree) with your advice note (packing note, invoice). some of the goods have been damaged in transport (transit).

d) We are awaiting your reply.
Please look into the matter and let us have your instructions.

III. *Errors*

a) We have received (we acknowledge) your letter (invoice, statement) of . . .

b) On checking your invoice (statement) we find that When comparing your invoice (your statement) with our order (with our books) we find that	you have charged quality XYZ at 95p instead of 85p. you show an invoice No. . . . for £28.70 of which we have no trace. you have listed (shown) your invoice No. . . . with £196.64 instead of £169.64. you have omitted your Credit Note No. . . . for £6.16.

c) Please look into the matter and if you agree kindly send us	a corrected invoice. a copy of your invoice No. . . . an adjusted (a corrected) statement.

d) We look forward to your (early) reply,

Apologies, Explanations and Adjustments

a) We acknowledge your letter (telephone call, telegram, cable) of . . .
We acknowledge the receipt of your letter (etc.) of . . .
We hasten to reply to your letter of . . .

b) I. *Delays*

We (very) much regret ⎫
We are very (extremely) ⎬ the delay in the delivery (despatch, execution, completion) of your order.
sorry about ⎭

The delay is due to causes beyond our control (to a strike, breakdown in the factory, shortage of raw material).

II. *Goods unsatisfactory or damaged*

We are (really) sorry to see (learn) from your letter
We are very sorry indeed

⎧ that you are not satisfied with our goods (delivery, shipment, consignment).
⎪ that you are complaining of the quality (weight, colour, finish) of . . .
⎨ that you say (think) that our goods (etc.) are not equal (up) to sample (standard).
⎪ that you think the price of . . . is too high (. . . is too expensive).
⎩ that our parcel (consignment, shipment) has been damaged in transit.

We have examined (gone into, looked into) the matter (your complaint) carefully (thoroughly).
We can assure you that our prices are in every respect competitive (are most carefully calculated, allow only a very small margin).
All our consignments are packed with the greatest possible care.

III. *Errors*

We (want to) express our (sincere) regret for
We offer our (sincere) apologies for
Please excuse
} the error (mistake) in our invoice (statement, shipment, consignment).

---

c) I. *Delays*

The goods (Your order) will be despatched tomorrow (next week, within a fortnight, before the end of the month).

We are making every effort to execute (despatch, complete) your order as soon as possible and hope to despatch it on...

As requested we have cabled you today as follows:

As requested we have (regretfully) cancelled your order.

II. *Goods unsatisfactory or damaged*

We are sending you today
} patterns (samples) of goods in stock.
Please select the pieces you want.
a range of lower priced articles and hope that some of these will meet your requirements (with your approval).

We have taken the matter up with the Post Office (Railway Company, Carrier) and would ask you to hold the goods at our disposal until you hear from us.

III. *Errors*

We are sending you herewith
We enclose
Please find enclosed
} our corrected invoice.
our Copy Invoice No. ....
our adjusted statement.
our Credit Note for the difference.

We are despatching the correct goods (the goods you ordered) and should be grateful if you would kindly return those sent in error.

---

d) We trust that the matter is now in order (has been settled to your satisfaction).

Please accept our (sincere) apologies for the delay (the error, the mistake) and the inconvenience (trouble) it has caused you.

Appendix II
Guide to Phonetic Transcription

Students of *Essential English* will be quite familiar with phonetic transcription; for others a very brief guide to the sounds and symbols is added here.

Phonetic Symbol	Examples	Phonetic Symbol	Examples
VOWELS		**DIPHTHONGS**	
iː	three, these, please	ei	say, train, plate
i	this, ship, shilling	ou	go, those, smoke
e	pen, desk, men	ai	five, side, eye
æ	man, hat, Paris	au	count, now, down
ɑː	calm, father, arm	ɔi	boy, noise, voice
ɔ	box, office, clock	iə	dear, clear, near
ɔː	all, small, draw	ɛə	where, chair, care
u	put, full, book	ɔə	four, door, floor
uː	two, move, blue	uə	sure, poor, tour
ʌ	up, much, come		
əː	third, word, earth		
ə	under, address, enter		

CONSONANTS

p	pen, pay, help	ʃ	ship, shilling, fish
b	be, boy, cab	ʒ	measure, pleasure
t	train, sit, stop	tʃ	Charles, each, much
d	day, word, Friday	dʒ	John, Japan, judge
k	keep, back, clock	h	his, here, unhappy
g	gold, good, dog	m	man, remain, swim
f	fine, safe, thief	n	name, finish, then
v	very, seven, leave	ŋ	thing, singing, working
θ	thank, nothing, fifth	r	red, around, very
ð	then, with, together	l	leave, pull, greatly
s	so, thinks, receive	w	will, away, wash
z	zero, has, noise	j	yellow, yes, new [njuː]

Stress is shown by a mark (′) put immediately before the syllable to be emphasised, e.g. [′hɔlədi] *holiday*, [mə′ʃiːn] *machine*, [′telifoun] *telephone*, [tə′lefənist] *telephonist*.

Index

Acceptance, 210
Advance Orders, 139
Advertising, 87
Agent, 87
Alarm Tab, 40
Applications for Job, 10-11, 53-8
Applications for Payment, 171ff.
Approval, on, 86

Bank Reference, 180-1
Banker's Discount, 213
Banker's Draft, 203
Bill of Exchange (B/E), 208ff.
Bill of Lading (B/L), 202ff., 225
Bonded Warehouse, 159

Calculating Machine, 151-2
Card Index, 24-9
Carriage Forward (Carr. fd.), 148
Carriage Paid (Carr. pd.), 148
Cash Discount, 76, 84, 184-5
Cash on Delivery (C.O.D.), 175, 203
Cash Paid Book, 163, 165
Cash Received Book, 163, 165
Cash with Order (C.W.O.), 175, 203, 224
Certified Invoice, 194-5
Chart, 188-9
Cheque, 208-9
Cipher, 138
Circular, 30
City, 1, 4, 212
Consular Invoice, 195, 225ff.
Copy Invoice, 171
Copy Order, 112
Cost, Insurance, Freight (C.I.F.), 196
Credit Limit, 179
Credit Status, 175, 212

Debt Collection Letters, 171ff.
Discount (Bill), 212-13
Discount (Cash), 76, 84, 184-5
Discount (Trade), 75, 84-5
Discount Tables, 151
Documents against Acceptance (D/A), 211ff.
Documents against Payment (D/P), 211ff.
Documentary Bill of Exchange, 211, 224ff.
Documentary Letter of Credit, 224ff.
Draft Terms, 203-4, 210ff., 225

Enquiries, 62ff.
Errors and Omissions Excepted (E.&O.E.), 148
Executive, 40

Filing Cabinet, 24

Firm Offer, 85
Free alongside Ship (f.a.s.), 196
Free on Board (f.o.b.), 195

Graph, 188

Inquiries, 62ff.
Insurance Policy, 225ff.
Inter-Com, 30
Irrevocable Letter of Credit, 224ff.

Letter of Credit (L/C), 222ff.

Mailing List, 26, 91
Mercantile Agency, 181

On Sale or Return, 128-9, 222
Order Book, 136
Order Form, 98ff.
Overcharge, 156

Paying-in Slip, 167
Petty Cash Book, 167
Postage Rates, 42
Price List, 67ff.
Pro Forma Invoice, 150, 175, 183, 196
Purchases Book, 137, 163-4
Purchases Ledger, 163-4

Quotation, 64ff.

Reference (Ref.), 46-7
References, 79, 110, 175ff., 212
Representative, 82

Sales Book, 163-7
Sales Ledger, 163-7
Sight Bill, 209ff.
Signal Tab, 27, 140
Statements, 170ff.
Status Inquiries, 175ff., 181-2, 212
Stencil, 30-1
Stock Control, 136ff.
Summary, 188
Sundry Accounts, 165
Switchboard, 35

Trade Discount, 75, 84-5
Trade References, 79, 110, 175, 212

Undercharge, 156
Usance Bill, 209ff.

Value Added Tax, 147

Writ, 182